LITTLECOTE, WILTSHIRE

ARCHAEOLOGICAL EXCAVATIONS IN THE PARK

## DEDICATION

The author would like to dedicate this book to his wife Andrea, and the excavation team: Bryn Walters, Peter Johnson, Luigi Thompson, Michael Barnard, and Geoffrey Shaddock, and the many volunteers who assisted on the site.

## ACKNOWLEDGEMENTS

The author would like to thank the two owners of Littlecote during the period which the excavation was undertaken. First Sir David Seton Wills for his support, financing, and enthusiasm, and secondly Peter de Savary for his continued support following his purchase of the estate. Also, the various estate workers who assisted in many ways the running of the excavation.

# Littlecote, Wiltshire

## Archaeological Excavations in the Park

### Bernard Phillips

THE HOBNOB PRESS

First published in the United Kingdom in 2022

by The Hobnob Press,
8 Lock Warehouse,
Severn Road, Gloucester GL1 2GA
www.hobnobpress.co.uk

© The Estate of Bernard Phillips, 2022

All rights reserved. No part of this book may be reprinted or reproduced or utilised in any form or by any electronic, mechanical or other means, now known or hereafter invented, including photocopying, or in any information storage or retrieval system, without the permission in writing from the copyright holders or their heirs.

British Library Cataloguing in Publication Data
A catalogue record for this book is available from the British Library

ISBN 978-1-914407-26-0

Typeset in Scala 11/14 pt.
Typesetting and origination by John Chandler

*Front cover: Excavating the Roman villa house*

*Back cover (main image): The sea monster on the mid fourth century Orpheus mosaic: Carnelian intaglio depicting Victory crowning Fortuna.*

# Contents

| | |
|---|---|
| *Dedication* | ii |
| *Acknowledgements* | ii |
| *Publisher's Note* | vi |
| *The Author* | vii |
| *Preface: an Appreciation of the Author, by Bryn Walters* | ix |
| *Illustrations* | xvi |

| | |
|---|---|
| 1. Introduction | 1 |
| 2. Geology and Setting | 4 |
| 3. Prehistoric 8,000 BC–500 BC | 6 |
| 4. Roman Military AD 45–60 | 8 |
| 5. Round House Settlement AD 60–100 | 11 |
| 6. Pseudo Villa AD 100-AD180 | 14 |
| 7. Stone Villa Complex AD 180-300 | 19 |
| 8. Villa Courtyard Complex AD 300-360 | 31 |
| 9. Orphic Complex AD 360-365 | 39 |
| 10. Decline and Decay AD 365-450 | 49 |
| 11. Saxon and Early Medieval Settlement AD 450-1150 | 55 |
| 12. Littlecote: a Medieval Village AD 1150-1450 | 60 |
| 13. Littlecote: a Medieval Village – The Archaeology AD 1150-1450 | 63 |
| 14. The Village and Villagers | 79 |
| 15. Post-Medieval Hunting Lodge AD1650-1780 | 91 |

| | |
|---|---|
| *References* | 111 |
| *Glossary* | 113 |
| *Places and People Index* | 119 |

## Publisher's Note

Bernard sent me the text and illustrations of this book in October 2021, some four weeks before his death on 15 November. There was no opportunity to discuss with him its contents or any aspect of its publication, although it followed in the wake of two previous books by him that I had published recently. I expected, therefore, to produce his Littlecote in a similar style to these, on which we had worked together, and of which he approved.

Had he lived I would have suggested that his text needed editing, and that he and I (or another editor) should work on it together to improve its flow and style. Since that has not been possible, and in view of the very detailed and meticulous descriptions of excavated structures, features and finds that Bernard has presented and have not been previously published, I have felt it best to retain, for the most part (and with the valued help of Peter Johnson and Mike Stone), the text as Bernard wrote it. We have, however, corrected spelling and grammar, and judiciously added punctuation to assist the reader wherever the meaning might be unclear. In a few places we have substituted words or reworked phrases. Beyond that I have left Bernard's text as I received it.

*John Chandler*
*Hobnob Press*

## The Author

Bernard Phillips, who died in 2021 shortly after completing this book, had been involved with archaeology in the area since the mid-1960s. Having joined the newly formed Swindon Archaeological Society he eventually became its Field Director. As such he directed and recorded excavations on Roman villas at Stanton Fitzwarren and Starveall Farm in Bishopstone Parish, other minor research excavations, conducted field walking and rescue excavations notably for the latter during construction of the M4 motorway, Stratton bypass and Lyncroft estate. In 1976 he joined an archaeological team who were excavating in Old Town, Swindon led by the then County Archaeologist, Roy Canham. This excavation on the site of Swindon House revealed much about Old Swindon's origins that evidently spanned a period of over ten thousand years. Most important was the discovery of Roman and Saxon buildings. During the summer of 1976 he acted as a supervisor for an archaeological excavation on a Roman town at Lower Wanborough. Returning to the Swindon House excavation he directed its final stages. Two further excavations followed in Old Town with him acting as director and recorder – Lloyds Bank in 1977 and Britannia Place in 1978. The former uncovered Roman remains and a Saxon hut, the latter a row of early nineteenth-century cottages. These excavations were conducted under the auspices of the County Archaeologist and Wiltshire Archaeological Society. Commencement of the archaeological excavation at Littlecote Park near Hungerford, with him acting as Excavation Director, began in 1978. Open to public viewing this long-term excavation (1978-1991) was paid for initially through the estate owner and subsequently became self-financing, having a museum, tearoom, educational facilities, and a gift shop. The excavation, initially aimed at a Roman villa discovered in the eighteenth century, revealed the site to be multi-period and resulted in the uncovering and recording of a Roman military invasion road, an early Roman settlement of circular huts, an almost entire Roman villa complex, a third of a medieval deserted village (tenth to fifteenth century), and a mid-seventeenth- to late eighteenth-century hunting

*The author recording a Roman well at Littlecote*

lodge along with its gardens and river frontage. Following the termination of the Littlecote excavation he undertook freelance archaeological work throughout much of Wiltshire, but chiefly in the Swindon area. This involved work for various companies and individuals as well as Wiltshire County Council Heritage and Libraries, and Swindon Borough Council. Amongst these was work on the Roman villa/temple site at Abbey Meads in North Swindon, the Saxon/medieval town of Cricklade, an Iron Age and Roman settlement at Calstone near Calne, a Mesolithic to Bronze Age occupation site at Kingsdown Crematorium, Neolithic pits at Whittonditch, and a walled eighteenth-century garden at Lydiard Park, Swindon.

## Preface
## an Appreciation of the Author
## BERNARD PHILLIPS
### by
### Bryn Walters
### Littlecote Project Director 1978 – 1991

In 1727, whilst digging post holes for a new fence around the hunting lodge, constructed beside the river Kennet in Littlecote Park near Ramsbury, the Steward of Littlecote William George discovered a very fine figured mosaic floor. He made a detailed drawing of it, alas now lost, but from which after he died his widow later made an elaborate embroidery in his memory. This hung in Littlecote House until 1985. It was also drawn by the Court artist George Vertue who produced a copper plate engraving of the pavement, the only known coloured copy of which is today preserved in the Bodleian Library in Oxford.

By 1730 the mosaic had been reburied as it was suffering from exposure to the elements and the land owner, Sir Francis Popham, declared the mosaic lost and gave a false location for it approximately a quarter of a mile west along the bridle path to Ramsbury. This was incorporated ultimately on the Ordnance Survey map of the area.

~~~

Bernard and I met for the first time in the early 1960s when the fledgling Swindon Archaeological Society was being formed. Bernard, along with his twin brother Roger, had already been undertaking field work reassessing known sites and discovering others across the Marlborough Downs and areas around Swindon. Working with Bernard at this time was my introduction to archaeology in the field, with Bernard meticulously keeping records and samples of recovered material.

Our collaboration grew rapidly over the following years working on rescue excavations at Lower Wanborough between 1966 and 1970.

These were initially directed by the late Ernest Greenfield on behalf of the then Ministry of Public Buildings and Works and later by John Wacher at Leicester University, who later became professor. It was at this time that Greenfield invited Bernard and me to join him on his excavations on the spectacular site at Great Witcombe in Gloucestershire, a site that would become extremely significant for me in the years to come. More locally, I joined Bernard in 1969 to undertake an exploratory excavation at Stanton Fitzwarren, two miles north-west of Swindon, along with other colleagues from the Swindon Society, to locate a long suspected large Roman villa alongside the embankment of the abandoned Swindon to Highworth railway. The investigation proved to be very successful. Again in 1972 we collaborated, along with his brother Roger, to identify and plot a lost villa on the downs south of the village of Bishopstone which again was successfully achieved. Bernard published the results in 1981.

Between 1969 and 1971 we were both heavily engaged in salvaging as much as possible from the sites being destroyed in the construction of the M4 Motorway. Most significantly the huge villa complex at Badbury, obliterated by interchange 15 and the Anglo-Saxon habitation site on the lower slopes of Liddington Hill near Medbourne. Bernard was to meet up with the Anglo-Saxons again when he was asked to undertake excavations at the rear of Old Town Square in Swindon, where he would reveal an amazing Saxon sunken-floored building, one of the best preserved ever found in England. These excavations continued to the east of High Street revealing Swindon's origin as an Anglo-Saxon community.

In 1970 I gave up my job as a sales manager to enrol in the Swindon School of Art and Design where I would meet my close friend, colleague and third member of the founding Littlecote triumvirate, Luigi Thompson. Whilst there I continued to collaborate on field work with Bernard and before too long Luigi joined us, his first major site being the extensive Roman potteries at Whitehill Farm in west Swindon which Bernard had discovered a year or so earlier. As the site was earmarked for housing development, on evidence supplied by Bernard, English Heritage financed a major excavation directed by Scott Anderson from Leicester University. The site proved to be very well preserved with at least 30 kilns being located by geophysical survey, only four of which were fully excavated along with a potters workshop. Consequently English Heritage put a preservation order on the site which is now a public recreational space, aptly named Kiln Park. Had it not been identified by Bernard's keen eye it may well have been totally destroyed. A second significant site saved from development was the large terraced complex on Groundwell Ridge in north Swindon where preliminary construction work for a housing estate was revealing Roman material. As I lived relatively nearby, I was contacted by the County Archaeological Officer, Roy Canham, who asked me to accompany him in an examination of the site and we soon determined there was something extensive there. Arrangements were made for Bernard and me to undertake trial sections on the site which was soon extended to larger scale operations revealing substantial structures. English Heritage agreed that the site was of National Importance and negotiated for it to be brought back into public ownership.

On graduation from Art School in 1974 I was persuaded by Dr Peter Fowler at Bristol to enter University College at Cardiff and study for a degree in archaeology. Luigi meanwhile joined 'CRAAGS' the 'Committee for Rescue Archaeology in Avon, Gloucestershire and Somerset' based in Bristol, as illustrator draughtsman and surveyor. Whilst at University I still continued during semester breaks and Bank Holiday weekends to work with Bernard exploring sites around the Roman towns at Mildenhall *(Minal)* near Marlborough, and Wanborough including aerial reconnaissance with our local businessman friend Bev Hill. It was during one of those flights in the great drought of 1976 that we located the amazing *Mansio (a Roman government rest house)* at the centre of the Roman town at Lower Wanborough. As he circled around the fields Bev said, "I think there's something down below which you will be interested in, hold on and look out of your windows as I tip the plane over on its side." As he did so Bernard and I looked straight down beneath the wing of the plane at the astounding feature below "Stop-Stop" I yelled, both of us being so excited at the image in the field. Bev circled around allowing Bernard to take oblique photos of the surrounding fields. The vertical photo (overleaf) secured by Bev's camera mounted through the floor of his cabin, remains one of the finest crop mark images of a Roman building ever taken. That was a day that neither of us would ever forget. We jointly published the discovery

*Crop mark of Roman Mansio at Lower Wanborough, Wiltshire*

in *Britannia*, the Roman Britain annual journal, the following year.

Bernard continued his research on Roman Wanborough plotting all known buildings and streets utilizing aerial images, producing as detailed a plan of Swindon's Roman town as possible. More detailed discussion on all the sites quoted above can be found in Bernard's book *The Archaeology of the Borough of Swindon* published in 2021.

The founding of the Littlecote Project, the subject of this volume, came about as a result of a set of unusual circumstances. On one of our flights with Bev Hill around the Marlborough Downs, looking for potential Roman sites and villas in particular for my university research project, his camera picked up some faint rectangular marks in the parkland west of Littlecote House near Ramsbury where, marked on the Ordnance Survey map of the area, a lost Roman mosaic was believed to be located. On returning to Cardiff I wrote to the Littlecote estate, the home of Sir Seton Wills, for permission to examine the area on the map and aerial photo, during a break from college. Within a week I received a reply from Sir Seton asking me to get in touch as soon as I was free and visit him at Littlecote House, as he was very interested indeed in locating the lost Roman building in his park. Soon after Bernard and I were entertained one evening by Sir Seton and we arranged a date and time to investigate the marks on the aerial photo. Come the day we drove up the field in a Land Rover with the gamekeeper to cut test holes in order to sample the underlying soil levels. Bernard, being Bernard, said "you carry on, I would prefer to take a closer look at those mounds under the trees down by the river," and off he trotted. After about an hour or so it became obvious that there was no evidence for there ever having been a Roman building at the location on the aerial photo. As we were back-filling and loading the tools into the Rover, I noticed Bernard coming up the slope towards us. I turned to Sir Seton and said "Ah, I think you will find that Bernard has found your lost villa" "What !" said Sir Seton "What makes you think that?" "Oh I know Bernard, he's taken his woolly cap off and he's carrying it in his hand and he's got one of his cheeky grins on his face."

As he reached us he asked "have you found anything ?" "No" I replied, "but you have haven't you!" I turned to Sir Seton saying, "Cup your hands together and I guarantee he will fill your palms with mosaic cubes". Sir Seton did as I suggested, as Bernard tipped his cap into Sir Seton's hands a cascade of Roman tesserae spilled into Seton's palms. That day Bernard sowed the seeds for the forthcoming Littlecote adventure and to this day Seton recalls the event as one of the most memorable of his experiences.

I had to finish my studies at university and, immediately after graduation, complete a commission for the Department of the Environment writing up the work done on the M4 in collaboration with Dr Peter Fowler. During this time Sir Seton Wills remained in regular contact asking me to make whatever arrangements were necessary to implement excavations at Littlecote. This meant putting together a full time team combined with accommodation, conservation laboratory, photographic studio and drawing office. In April 1978 Sir Seton funded a long term research project until he sold the estate in 1985 to the entrepreneur Mr Peter de Savary who continued to support the project to its completion in 1991.

I was engaged as administrative Project Director but there was only one person I wanted to take charge of the physical archaeology and compilation of records – Bernard Phillips, who gladly accepted as Archaeological Director along with my colleague from Art School Luigi Thompson, then at C.R.A.A.G.s in Bristol, as Draughtsman, Illustrator and Surveyor. The three of us were the founding triumvirate of the Littlecote Project. Peter Johnson, then a post-graduate studying Romano-British mosaics at Newcastle, joined the team later, in July 1978, then full-time from 1980 as Assistant Archaeological Director.

The basic rationale behind the venture was to identify a Roman villa that had not completely died out with the end of the Roman Empire but had continued, through succeeding ages, as a focus for an agricultural community centred on a Patron's residence. The present day *villa domus* being the great Tudor mansion of Littlecote House. Such communities having been identified on the continental mainland where villas became villages. Remains of villas are frequently identified adjacent to or underlying early churches, occasionally the church being constructed on original Roman foundations. The church substituting as the focus for a community around which villages would slowly develop.

*Bernard Phillips (left) and his brother Roger (right)*

A further aspect of the Littlecote project was that, upon the completed excavation of an area within which a major building was sited, its remains would be consolidated for permanent display. Exceptionally for a villa excavation, the structural conservation would be undertaken by the excavation team, overseen by Bernard. Unlike seasonal excavations, work was undertaken every day throughout the year. We remained at Littlecote as a full time team for 13 years from 1978 to 1991 with many volunteers over that period, two of whom went on to university to gain archaeological degrees. Over that time I calculated that around a million people visited the site. It remains one of the most significant villa excavations ever undertaken in this country.

A great highlight was the production of BBC 2's *Chronicle* documentary about the excavations 'Orpheus and the Gentleman Farmer' which was first screened in April 1981. It gained the highest number of viewers in that season's run of films, overtaking that on the lifting of 'The Mary Rose'.

After Littlecote Bernard established his own archaeological consultancy, undertaking many pre-development contracts. Tragically during this time his brother Roger died in May 2006, a terrible blow as, being twins, they were extremely close. In recent years Bernard also took to writing, compiling historical accounts on archaeology in north Wiltshire, much of it in collaboration with his friend Mogs Boon who also sadly passed away in 2021. They worked together on Bernard's books, including this the third volume, on the excavations in Littlecote Park. The publication of this work is a fitting tribute to an excellent archaeologist and true gentleman who is greatly missed by his family and many friends and associates. With Bernard's passing a light has gone out in my life as I have lost a great colleague and true friend.

*BRYN WALTERS*
*The Association for Roman Archaeology.*

# Illustrations

**Fig. 1.** Littlecote House
**Fig. 2.** Littlecote House viewed from the River Kennet
**Fig. 3.** Littlecote excavation showing the various historical periods superimposed, after five years of excavation
**Fig. 4.** Neolithic flint arrowheads from Littlecote
**Fig. 5.** The Roman road and its drainage ditches
**Fig. 6.** Roman cavalry horse mount from Littlecote
**Fig. 7.** Silver Dobunnic coin from Littlecote
**Fig. 8.** Early military features AD 45-60
**Fig. 9.** Circular huts and enclosure AD 60-100
**Fig. 10.** Riverside chalk-floored round house
**Fig. 11.** Charred grain from the riverside building
**Fig. 12.** Pseudo villa complex AD 100-180
**Fig. 13.** Timber steeping tank c. AD 100 in the riverside building
**Fig. 14.** Decorated Samian ware bowl from Littlecote
**Fig. 15.** Villa complex AD 180
**Fig. 16.** Work hall and domestic wing
**Fig. 17.** Villa house AD 180
**Fig. 18.** Villa House Remains
**Fig. 19.** Villa house kitchen
**Fig. 20.** Villa well
**Fig. 21.** Drier foundations c. AD 180
**Fig. 22.** Villa complex c. AD 230
**Fig. 23.** Silver ring set with an intaglio depicting the god Sol from Littlecote
**Fig. 24.** Carnelian intaglio from Littlecote depicting Victoria crowning Fortuna
**Fig. 25.** Bronze smelting furnace in the villa house
**Fig. 26.** Villa complex c. AD 300
**Fig. 27.** Villa house AD 360
**Fig. 28.** Gold betrothal ring found in the villa house

Fig. 29. The gatehouse foundations
Fig. 30. The villa gatehouse reconstruction
Fig. 31. Riverside barn
Fig. 32. Orphic complex c. AD 365
Fig. 33. The riverside Orphic building
Fig. 34. Orpheus mosaic following relaying and restoration
Fig. 35. Bronze dividers from the Orphic building
Fig. 36. Orpheus on the mosaic
Fig. 37. Busts of Bacchus and Antinous from Littlecote
Fig. 38. Interior of the Orphic Hall
Fig. 39. Villa c. AD 420
Fig. 40. Building demolition debris in the south building's bath house stoke pit
Fig. 41. Late Roman/post-Roman burial from behind the southern building
Fig. 42. Liddington Castle an Iron Age hillfort refortified in the post-Roman period
Fig. 43. Saxon bone bobbin from Littlecote
Fig. 44. Part of a wooden bucket from the tenth-century well
Fig. 45. Tenth-century well at Littlecote
Fig. 46. The earthworks of the medieval village
Fig. 47. The village c. AD 1200
Fig. 48. The village c. AD 1400
Fig. 49. Longhouse (Bld. 2), plot A
Fig. 50. Longhouse (Bld. 4), plot B
Fig. 51. Sunken floored building (Bld. 9) plot C
Fig. 52. Farmhouse (Bld. 8), plot C
Fig. 53. Well, plot D
Fig. 54. Sheepcote (Bld. 11), plot D
Fig. 55. Store/workshop (Bld. 15), plot D
Fig. 56. House (Bld. 17), plot D showing bread oven, hearth, and malting oven
Fig. 57. Cess pit in Bld. 18, plot D
Fig. 58. Building 18, plot D
Fig. 59. Bread oven, plot E
Fig. 60. Cat and mouse, Luttrell Psalter c. 1325
Fig. 61. Smithy as illustrated in a medieval manuscript

Fig. 62. Bread oven as illustrated in a medieval manuscript
Fig. 63. Iron candlestick, as discovered
Fig. 64. Early fourteenth-century 'Kennet Valley' jug from a well in plot D
Fig. 65. A timber-built sheepcote, Book of Hours of Duc de Berry 1409-16
Fig. 66. Store/workshop (Bld. 5), plot B
Fig. 67. English School, oil painting of house and hunting park c. 1730
Fig. 68. The hunting lodge c. 1760
Fig. 69. The hunting lodge phases of construction
Fig. 70. Excavated house on the c. 1730 oil painting
Fig. 71. Early eighteenth-century Delft ware chamber pot from the river
Fig. 72. Remains of the seventeenth-/eighteenth-century cottage/hunting lodge
Fig. 73. Seals from wine bottles from the river
Fig. 74. Late seventeenth-century leather shoe from the river
Fig. 75. Carved bone comb, whistle, and apple corer from the river
Fig. 76. Early eighteenth-century wood and iron mouse trap from the river
Fig. 77. Watch key, jaws harps, tweezers, penknife, and a fob with seal from the river
Fig. 78. Clay pipes c. 1650 to 1700 from the river
Fig. 79. Lead strip depicting a stag's head from the river
Fig. 80. Popham coat-of-arms
Fig. 81. Littlecote Park shown on a map of Wiltshire by Robert Morden 1695
Fig. 82. Littlecote Park shown on a map of Wiltshire by Andrews and Dury, 1773
Fig. 83. Mary George's embroidery of the Orpheus mosaic
Fig. 84. Alexander Popham (1605-1669) and his family

# I
# Introduction

Littlecote House is a large Tudor mansion that has been much added to over the ensuing centuries, even into the 1990s when it was taken over by Warner Leisure Hotels. It lies in Wiltshire, close to the Berkshire border, on the River Kennet's southern bank. The walled gardens at the rear stretch from the house to a former course of the river that was diverted further north, apparently in the early eighteenth century. Around the house and gardens lie areas of grassed and wooded parkland, and beyond that there is farmland, and water meadows.

Fig. 1. *Littlecote House*

It was in 1727 in the park beneath his cottage's vegetable patch that William George, Littlecote's estate steward, made an amazing discovery that had been hidden on the south bank of the River Kennet for many centuries. It was a discovery that was to be repeated exactly two hundred and fifty years later when two archaeologists, Bryn Walters and Bernard Phillips, ventured into the park in search of William's long-lost

*Fig. 2. Littlecote House viewed from the River Kennet*

discovery, a fabulous Roman mosaic. Its finding had caused much interest at the time of its initial discovery, having been noted in the minutes of the Society of Antiquaries of London in April 1728. The Marquis of Hertford, a member of the Society, was so impressed that he commissioned the artist George Vertue to produce drawings of the floor. Prints of Vertue's work remained, along with an embroidery stitched by William's wife Mary, as the only original illustration available for the mosaic as, shortly after its discovery, the floor was stated to have been destroyed. Indeed, not long after that William's cottage was demolished, and the Roman floor's location forgotten. Bernard and Bryn with the owner of the estate, Sir David Seton Wills, walked into a ploughed field where aerial photographs had shown marks that could relate to a Roman building. However, from the lack of Roman debris on the field surface it soon became clear that no building had existed there. On the way to the field the two archaeologists had noted earthworks extending alongside a watercourse. Bernard seized the opportunity to examine these remains and there in soil dug out of a burrow by rabbits he found Roman tesserae – cubes of stone and tile that made up Roman mosaic floors. William's Roman building site had been rediscovered some 400 yards (365 metres) west of Littlecote House. The following year Bryn, assisted by friends, undertook the cutting of a few small trenches and, astonishingly, uncovered parts of William George's floor which had survived some 30cms below the surface. Pottery and other finds found showed that not only a Roman site existed here but also a medieval village and a post-medieval building, the cottage that had been William's home. This rediscovery prompted Sir Seton Wills to offer to finance the site's excavation. The presence of the manor's existing tourist and educational facility encouraged Bryn and Bernard to accept the offer. Over the following months a team of archaeologists and a conservationist were put together to undertake the work and they were to be ably assisted by many volunteers over the succeeding years. It rapidly became clear that here an opportunity existed to undertake a thorough long-term investigation of a multi-period rural site which would hopefully be a permanent self-financing leisure and educational amenity for the public. In 1978, prior to the commencement of the excavation the existing earthworks, which stretched alongside the former river course for six hundred and fifty metres, were surveyed by the archaeological team.

Eventually more than one hectare of ground was excavated. Initially the funding of the work came from Sir Seton Wills. Following the sale of Littlecote in October 1985 to Mr Peter de Savary the project continued and was supported by him until April 1990. The final stage to April 1991 of the project was completed under the auspices of the newly formed Roman Research Trust and was self-financing with income being generated from an on-site gift shop and cafeteria. The house and surrounding grounds were sold to Warner Leisure in 1996 for use as a hotel.

*The excavation team comprised Bryn Walters (Director); Bernard Phillips (Excavation Director); Peter Johnson (Assistant Site Director); Luigi Thompson (Site Draughtsman, Photographer, and Illustrator); Michael Barnard and Geoffrey Shaddock (Site Workers); Margaret Roberts B.Sc. and Jan Drake (Conservators). A site office and other facilities were established above the former Littlecote stable block. The excavation team was helped by many volunteers amongst whom where John Hamblin, Rod Jones, Howard Gibbs, Tony May, Stan Ford, John Deacon, John and Jean Clapton, Richard and Mandy Akehurst, Ian Selby, Simon Marshal, Philip Fox, Paul Cannon, Sarah Ward, Damian de Rosa, Simon Pope and David Reeves.*

# 2
# Geology and Setting

Where the archaeological excavation site lies, on the south side of a valley through which the River Kennet flows on its way to join the River Thames near Reading, only a narrow tract of level ground exists before it rises 60 metres quite steeply. On the opposite side of the river and its meadow lands the ground rises gently to a similar height.

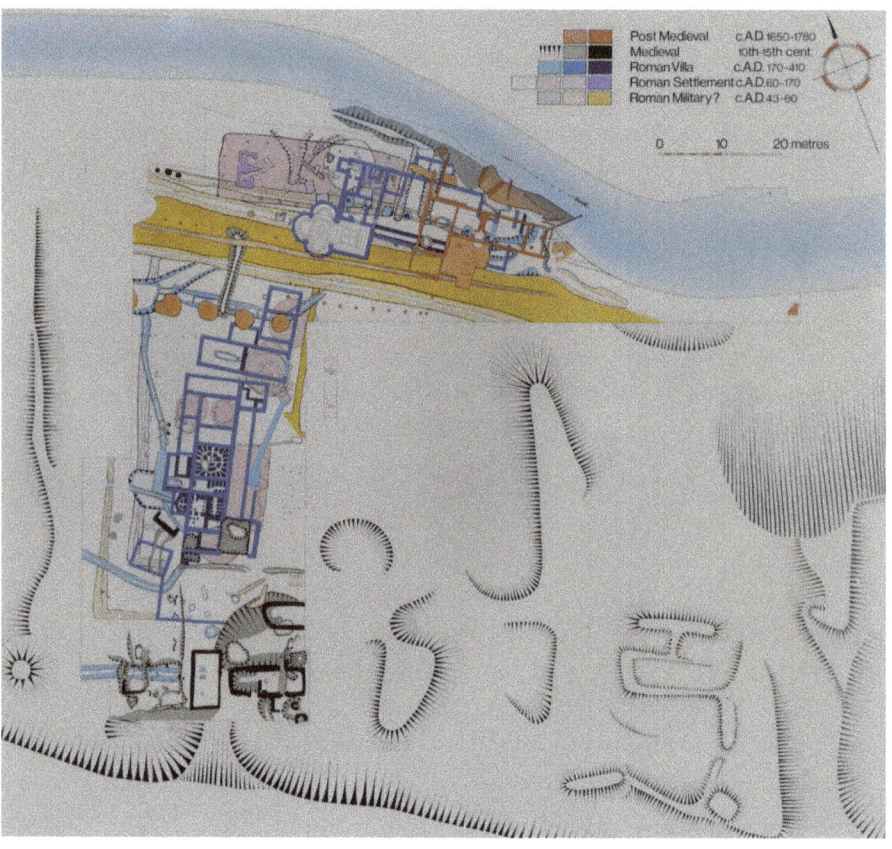

*Fig. 3. Littlecote excavation showing the various historical periods superimposed, after five years of excavation*

The underlying geology comprises upper chalk – a soft white stone containing bands of flint nodules – overlain by a range of deposits laid down in the Ice Age (the *Pleistocene* era) which lasted from about 2,588,000 to 11,700 years ago. They include clay and flints, tertiary debris, river and valley gravel, and alluvium. Filling in channels and forming beds over the gravel are more recent deposits of peat and fullers' earth. Overlying soils (*rendzinas*) formed from the underlying chalk base are mostly shallow, humus-rich, loamy, and flinty.

# 3
# Prehistoric (8,500-500 BC)

Excavation soon revealed that the gravel terrace on the south side of the River Kennet at Littlecote had first seen human activity many thousands of years ago with the finding of over three hundred worked flint tools and pieces of flint-working waste. Included were arrowheads; scrapers; blades and flakes, some serrated and notched; cores, from which blades and flakes were struck using hammer stones or punches; and microliths – tiny re-worked blades that combined and set in wood formed items such as arrows, harpoons, scythes and scouring blocks. Based on the types, forms and manufacturing techniques employed in their making it could be seen that they span the Upper Palaeolithic to the Bronze Age, extending over a total of ten thousand years or more. Many flints came from the gravel and silty clay layers laid down by the river and which predated the Roman deposits. Other flints and a few Late Bronze Age and Early Iron Age pottery sherds were residual and came from later period contexts.

*Fig. 4. Neolithic flint arrowheads from Littlecote*

*The British Paleolithic is a record of intermittent human occupation commencing over 800,000 years ago, divided by episodes when advancing ice sheets, up to two miles thick, caused the countryside to be abandoned. Open tundra with little forest development was grazed upon by horse, red deer, mammoth, rhino, reindeer, arctic hare, saiga antelope, and wild cattle and hunted upon by brown bear, lynx, hyena, fox, and wolf. The early humans roamed over the land, hunting the migrating animals for food and clothing and they occupied shelters made of animal skins and timber. About 11,800 years ago increasing woodland growth caused a decline in the animal' traditionally hunted so new tool types that suited the hunting of the incoming animal species were made. Around 8,000 BC, signalling the Mesolithic era, temperatures rose to those like today. Thick forests of birch, hazel, oak, elm, lime, alder, and pine, only broken by water courses, lakes, marshland, and mountain tops, now stretched from one end of Britain to the other. In these wildwoods deer, wild cattle, boar, wild pig, elk, beaver, wolf, wild cat, brown bear, otter, pine marten and a variety of bird life existed. Small groups of hunters and gatherers occupied overnight or seasonal camps or long-term bases with substantial round timber framed buildings. A growing population meant a shortage of hunting and gathering resources and heralded the need for a new way to source food. Farming introduced from the Continent arrived at the start of the Neolithic period around 4,100 BC. Woodland was cleared to provide land for the growing of crops and pasture for herds of cattle and pig. Within the clearings rectangular post-built houses were erected. Surrounding woodland was foraged for timber and for hazel nuts, edible roots, berries, fungi, tubers, and crab apples. Settlement became permanent and moving was only a necessity when land became infertile or resources in the adjacent woodland were exhausted. Tribal territories appear to have been established marked by earthen monuments – ditched enclosures that defined special places for ritual, trading or multi-tribal gatherings, and earthen burial mounds were places of change, a connection between the living and the spirit world. Recent DNA evidence shows that in about 2,500 BC incoming people had rapidly replaced the indigenous population. These newcomers who signify the commencement of the Bronze Age have been given the name 'Beaker people' due to the highly decorated drinking vessels found in their graves.*

# 4
# Roman Military (AD 45-60)

In 43 AD the Roman military invaded Britain. Following the primary objective of the Emperor Claudius's army – the capture of the Catuvellaunian tribal capital at Camulodunum (Colchester) and

*Fig. 5. The Roman road and its drainage ditches*

subjugation of the tribe – attention turned to pacifying the rest of Southern Britain. Vespasian, a future emperor, led the Legion II Augusta westward subduing tribes and capturing oppida as they went. Such a military force would have required the building of roads to keep it supplied with equipment, food, and fresh troops, as well as enabling the sending back of captives, injured personnel, and tributes. Within the Kennet Valley extending through the excavation site a 7.3-metres-wide gravelled road with shallow side ditches and a northern marker ditch was discovered. Stratification and dating evidence show that it was built to serve the

Fig. 6. *Roman cavalry horse mount from Littlecote*

legion's advance. Continuing along the Kennet Valley the road would subsequently have reached the probable site of a fort at Mildenhall (*Cvnetio*), or by crossing the river at Littlecote the road could have extended along the Ald Valley into *Dobunnic* tribal territory and the likely fort site at Lower Wanborough (*Durocornovium*) and thence on to the cavalry fort located at Cirencester (*Corinium*). At Littlecote, south of the road, traces of a significant timber structure and a latrine pit may have been part of a military camp that was stationed here to protect the road and perhaps an adjacent river crossing, and to police the native populace. It could also have been located here at a point at which embarkation and disembarkation of river-borne transportation could have taken place, particularly for the shipment of procured native-produced grain and livestock needed to supply troops at a base camp down river at Silchester (*Calleva*

Fig. 7. *Silver Dobunnic coin from Littlecote*

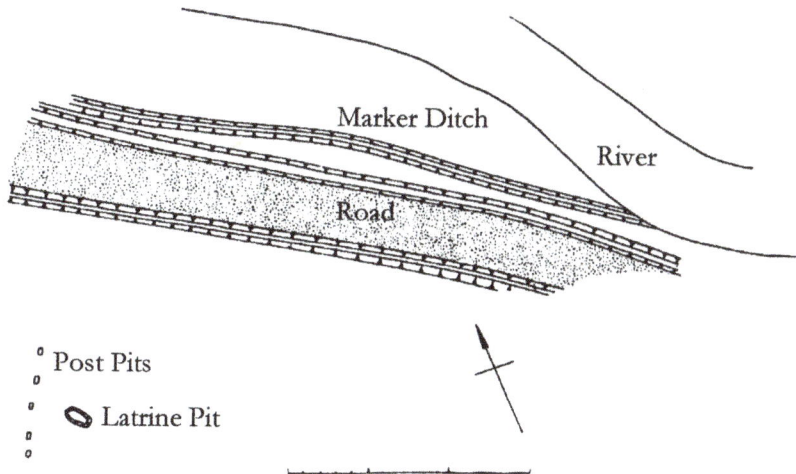

Fig. 8. *Early military features AD 45-60*

*Atrebatum*). It has been noted (Griffiths 2001) that a high incidence of cavalry-related finds compared to infantry items occur on the Wiltshire Downs. It is suggested that these items are the result of deployment of horse soldiers in the open countryside whilst foot soldiers were largely deployed where siege warfare was needed. One object found adjacent to the road at Littlecote is a bronze cavalry harness mount. Other finds of the period from the excavation are a *Dobunnic* silver coin inscribed ANTED, which is datable to the last decade before the Roman conquest; a coin of Caligula with a counter stamp of Claudius (typical of military issue); sherds of Claudian/Neronian Samian ware and a mid first-century bronze brooch.

How long the possible military base remained at Littlecote is unclear but the need to reinforce one timber post could mean it was for years. The timber structures were deliberately dismantled, the post sockets packed with water-worn pebbles and the latrine pit infilled with soil. Animal bones from the latter's infilling show that the site's occupants dined chiefly on mutton but also on beef and pork.

# 5
# Round House Settlement (AD 60-100)

The site was not abandoned for long as an extensive enclosure ditch was dug, its northern side being the road's southern drainage ditch. Only partly excavated the enclosure contained at least four circular chalk-floored and seemingly clay-walled huts, three having central hearths. The fourth may have been used for storage. In association were two external ovens and a grain storage pit which showed that these buildings were for domestic occupation. A much larger isolated clay-walled circular hut lay on the opposite side of the road adjacent to the river and was accessed by a paved ford built across the road's two northern ditches. This contained a big central fire pit and an oven. The layout within the enclosure appears regimented with huts being confined to the outer

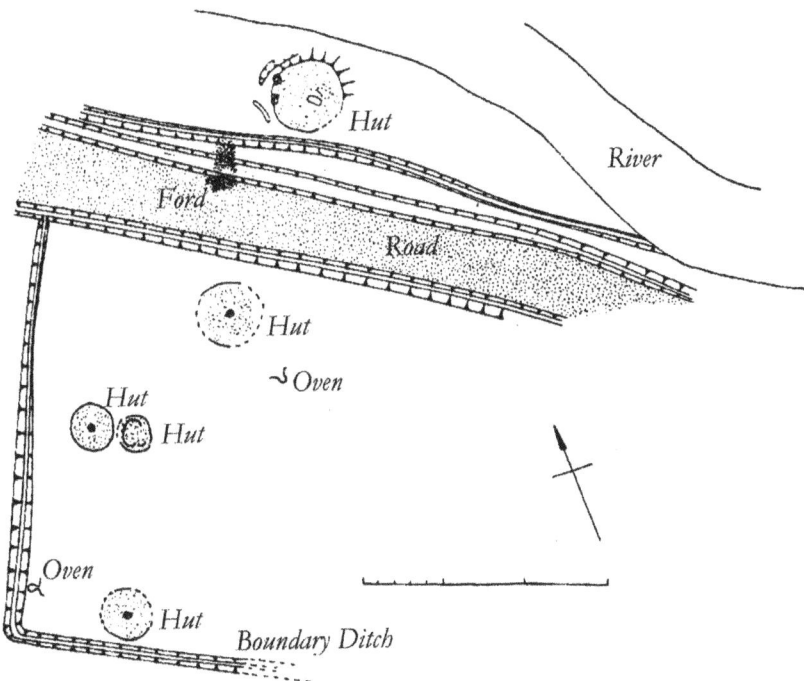

Fig. 9. *Circular huts and enclosure AD 60-100*

edges of the enclosure without apparent divisions between them and uniform in construction. This arrangement could indicate housing for workers with an absent estate owner, or one living in a larger structure yet unexcavated rather than individuals farming their own plots. This may account for the structures' relatively small size which represented a change from traditional communal living along with all the families' goods, animals, and equipment, to a servile family with few goods and with farming equipment kept elsewhere.

As to the settlement's function it is the riverside hut that provides some clues. Its large central fire-pit is of unusual form – rectangular with rounded ends and indications of an upper structure. This and the presence within its ash fill of charred wheat grain hint at its use as a malting hearth/kiln. Charred grain was also present in the adjacent oven. That the hearth and oven were in regular use is revealed by abundant discarded ash incorporating charred grain and chaff that partly filled the building's external drainage gullies and spread for some distance along the river edge. Eventual demolition of this building was followed directly by the construction over it of a large, channelled drier associated with more charred grain signifying continued crop production and probably malt production.

*Fig. 10. Riverside chalk-floored round house*

There has been much discussion on the use of so-called 'corn driers' since experiments had indicated that they were not very effective for that singular use (Reynolds and Langley 1979). It is very likely that they were multi-functional, being used to dry grain and other commodities (i.e., flax, beans, peas, cheese, and sausage), and for parching and roasting grain (Morris 1979). The latter would have been part of the process for making malt (Halbaek 1964). Adapted and enclosed they could also be used for smoking food such as meats and fish. Most driers are found on villa sites or rural settlements and their use in Britain dates from the late first century, but they are chiefly of the fourth century (Morris 1979).

Apart from the potential malt production evidence on the settlement site of agricultural or industrial activity is slight. It comprises the grain, a few quern-stone fragments, a whetstone, a few iron-slag lumps, and pieces of handmade tiles of a type thought to have been used in ovens, or their construction (Mepham 1993). The grain, chiefly spelt wheat, and a little barley, found in and around the riverside hut clearly implies crop cultivation. Animal bones recovered also indicate livestock rearing – mainly of sheep/goat, but also of cattle and pig. Of note, found close to the riverside hut within the lower fill of the road's boundary ditch, a bronze stylus implies literacy and record-keeping. Most of the pottery fragments found are from coarseware bowls, jars, and dishes, all produced on local kiln sites. A few imported fine-ware vessels are also represented though, chiefly beakers, dishes, and platters imported from Gaul.

Fig. 11. Charred grain from the riverside building

# 6
# Pseudo Villa (AD 100-180)

Around AD 100 levelling of the circular huts and infilling of the enclosure ditch occurred. Set in a rectangular, palisaded enclosure and accessed from the road via a timber bridge constructed over the road's south drainage ditch and a gravel-surfaced flint-block path, two buildings were then erected. Built nearly central to the enclosure, an 8-metre by 15-metre rectangular chalk and gravel-floored structure incorporated a hearth and ovens. At the north end a drain exited the building, implying that it could also have housed animals, much like a medieval longhouse. Consequently it is likely that internal divisions had

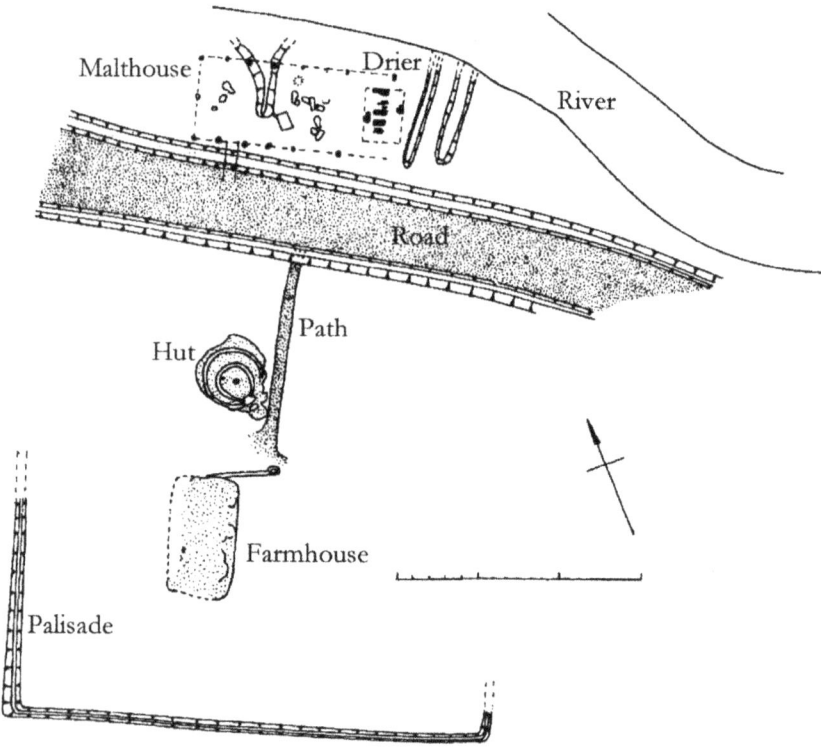

Fig. 12. Pseudo villa complex AD 100-180

existed. Lack of structural evidence points to walls constructed of wattle and daub set into sill beams resting on and around the flooring, while the lack of stone or terracotta roof tiles indicates thatch or shake/shingle roofing. Adjacent to its northern end a circular structure had a porch facing south-east and a central hearth. Clearly created by load-bearing walls, two continuous non-concentric circular channels, one inside the other, were evidenced compressed into its chalk floor. The inner ring lay quite close to the outer, adjacent to the porch entrance. Both had clearly defined thresholds that faced the porch. The unusual plan presented by this building creates difficulties in defining its internal construction and function. The outer circle being deeper and wider was clearly the main load-bearing wall, whilst the inner may have supported a screen or was low in height, perhaps supporting a platform which extended around the interior. Four options can be proposed for the structure's use; domestic, smokehouse, sweat lodge or ritual. Domestic because of the presence of the central fire pit, a smokehouse owing to the function of the building which later replaced it, a sweat house owing to the fire pit and potential internal platform, and finally ritual due to the unusual layout.

Across the road, accessed by a timber footbridge and the ford built across the road's northern drainage ditch a 9.5-metres by 23.5-metres timber building incorporated, at its east end, the channelled drier of the previous phase. Constructed adjacent to the river and floored with clay its wall posts and attached

Fig. 13. Timber steeping tank c. AD 100 in the riverside building

roof beams were supported by large, carefully levelled sarsen stones implying that the upper structure was prefabricated. Features within the building included a large timber tank and eight clay-walled ovens. It is likely that due to the nature of the internal features it was, at least in part, open-sided to allow the exit of smoke from the ovens and drier. Finds comprised both quern-stone and large storage jar fragments, and carbonised grain. The grain, chiefly hulled wheat and some barley, included some that had germinated. The timber tank's lower part was well preserved with the plank floor being nailed from beneath showing that it had been assembled before setting it into the ground. Its wall timbers were fixed with tongue and slot joints held by pegs inserted from below. This tank's function, when taken in association with the other elements within the building (ovens, drier, grain, and quern stones) and the adjacent river as a water source, was clearly that of a steeping tank, used in malt-making. Malt was evidently being made on a large scale.

While there is no unmistakable evidence that, following the making of the malt, the production of beer took place it is feasible that it did as the necessary items of quern-stones, ovens, water, and large storage jars were present. In the brewing process milling of the malted grain was followed by mashing – mixing milled malted grain with water and heating. Next lautering – separating the resultant mash from the liquid wort and the residual grain – then by boiling, fermenting, maturing/ageing, filtering, and finally placing into casks. Military and domestic wooden tablets excavated at *Vindolanda* (a fort near Hadrian's Wall), dated AD 90 to AD 130, which was about the time of the erection of the Littlecote building, reveal that the fort's garrison purchased beer

---

*In the making of malt the grain would have been first soaked in a steeping pit for a day or two. Shortly after covering with water the grains swell and increase in size. Following draining of the tank transference of the grain to a temporary wooden platform took place. Here, piled 30cm to 40cm high, the grains would begin to generate heat and germinate. After a day or two they were spread out onto a growing floor sufficiently deep to encourage more growth. Then, following turning at intervals over fourteen days or so and gradually spreading thinner to achieve even growth, the sprouted grains were moved to a drier and spread 10cm to 15cm deep. Initially a gentle fire would have been started and gradually increased over two to four days to suit the malt's purpose and the desired colour. The grain was then sieved to remove the shoots. The resulting malted grain would then have been ready for milling, prior to use in beer production.*

from local brewers. Another product that could have been produced within the Littlecote building, hinted at by the many ovens and quernstones, is bread, which could have been on a large scale. Yeast, being a biproduct of the brewing process, could have been used as an ingredient in its production.

Plainly, malted grain or milled malt, and possibly beer and bread production within the riverside building, would have been substantial, on a scale much above that needed for the settlement's needs, thus outlets for the produce must have existed. Several options are presented – either sale through a local market, to a market trader, to a military commissariat or, if the military road remained in general use, it could be that the buildings during this phase and the previous one, functioned as a wayside hostelry. Located halfway between the Roman towns of *Spinis* (Speen) and *Cvnetio* (Mildenhall) Littlecote would have been a convenient stopping point at which military and civilian travellers could halt and purchase food and drink. A link between such brewing activities and travellers and roadside settlements has been suggested (Stevens et al 2011).

Transportation by road in the Roman world was slow and expensive, particularly over long distances, due to the need for feeding and housing animals, carters, and drovers. At Littlecote, where the sarsen padded building and subsequent driers and barns lay on the river edge, a further option for transporting produce may have been by river. Water transportation was presumably cheaper, quicker, and less congested. It could be that the villa's grain, malt, ale, and other products were transported in this manner. It is feasible that shallow draught vessels under oar, sail, or poled could reach upstream as far as the Roman town of *Cvnetio*, which lies on the Kennet's southern bank, 9-kilometres upstream of Littlecote, or downstream to where the river joins the River Thames at Reading. It has been suggested that at that point a river port for the cantonal capital *Calleva* (Silchester) existed (Rivet 1964) as there is considerable evidence of Roman activity in and around the modern town. Two shallow, parallel ditches uncovered at the end of the riverside building could have been used for narrow shallow draught vessels to be drawn up for loading with the building's produce. The adjacent gently sloping area enclosed by low banks and ditches and on which river silting was evidenced, could have been used for repairing and storage of boats when not required.

*Fig. 14. Decorated Samian ware bowl from Littlecote*

As a further source of wealth some stock rearing was undertaken. Based on bone identification, animals consumed on the site now show a rise, over the previous phase, in beef production at the expense of sheep, whilst pig produce stayed relatively the same. However, based on the nature of the riverside building, much land must have been given over to grain production.

Imported vessels displayed on the inhabitants' tables included colour-coated beakers from the Argonne region and Cologne, and North Gaulish Samian ware demonstrating the inhabitants' desire to display the trappings of accrued wealth. Wealth is also demonstrated by glass vessels which include cups, beakers, bowls, and jugs.

# 7
# Stone Villa Complex (AD 180-300)

Twenty-eight coins found pre-date AD180. These support, along with imported pottery, the archaeological evidence that following the military phase the rural native settlement and the following farmstead had flourished. This prosperity enabled in about AD 180 the construction of a courtyard complex recognisable as the centre of a Romanised estate. Forming the western side of the complex, on the south side of the road, three contemporary stone buildings were erected over the remains of the demolished farmhouse and circular building. Here builders' activity is shown by the finding of an exceptionally large gravel pit, mounds of constructional material and a mortar mixing area. Some of these pre-dated the main southern building's construction, indicating that the

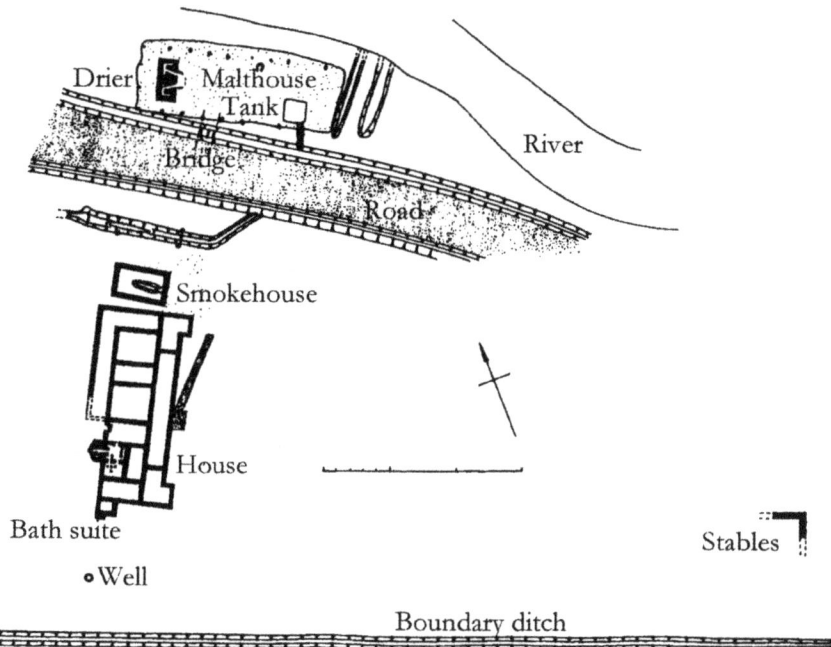

Fig. 15. Villa complex AD 180

northern building was erected first. This flint-block building measured 5-metres by 8-metres and is identifiable as a smokehouse due to the presence of an internal long hearth and the building's height. A height that could be determined as its southern side wall fell intact two hundred and fifty years later. Corbelling stones on top showed that the wall had stood 6-metres high so the overall height of this structure must have been around 8-metres. Fired external to the building, smoke travelled along the long hearth's covered channel into the building's centre where upon exiting it rose amongst the produce being smoked, hung on high wooden racks. Littlecote's smokehouse is apparently the first identified

*Fig. 16. Work hall and domestic wing*

as such in Roman Britain. The purpose of a smokehouse was not only to accentuate food taste but, mainly, for long term preservation. This was achieved firstly by salt-curing and then prolonged smoking using cold smoke. Roman literature refers to smoked cheese, sausage, and pork (Morris 1979), and undoubtedly many other food types were also treated in this way. On the building's northern side linking with the road's southern drainage ditch a deep linear cutting incorporated a deeper section set between timber sluice gates. Clearly this served as a retention pool, adding further credence for the building's use. Here fish, following capture in traps placed in the river, could be retained prior to gutting, and curing. If fish were to be cold smoked it was necessary to undertake this quickly while the fish were still wet so limiting bacterial growth. Evidence for fish farming (*pisciculture*) in Roman Britain appears to be virtually non-existent although evidence for fish consumption is widespread (Locker 2007). Fish bones – notably eel – from Littlecote's house kitchen and in the midden to the rear confirm that fish was part of the occupants' diet. It seems that the smokehouse soon fell into disuse though the structure was extended eastward to create a 5-metres by 15-metres single roomed building floored in mortar. During its life it incorporated a series of hearths as well as three infant burials, a ritual sheep burial and bronze-smelting furnaces. Approached by a slight ramp a wide eastern entrance suggests that the extended structure served as a workshop. In this building the repair and manufacture of farming equipment and other items would have taken place. It is likely that the building had an upper floor for the accommodation of the building's workers. Later they were also provided for by an addition erected on the workshop's northern side that comprised two rooms, the eastern of which contained another infant burial. It was later replaced with a much more substantial 10.5-metres by 5.9-metres wing that incorporated a corridor and two rooms. The southern room had centrally a tiled hearth and the other room had in its south-western corner a further infant burial.

The second building erected south of the smokehouse measured 29-metres by 12.3-metres and was of a 'winged corridor house' type, so named as rooms extended outwards at both ends. Access into this type of building was via a central doorway in the front corridor that often had an outer porch, as did the Littlecote villa house. On its ground floor it initially comprised two rooms divided by a corridor and a north wing

*Fig. 17. Villa house AD 180*

*Roman bathing involved progressing through rooms of differing heat. From the undressing room (apodyterium) the bathers entered a warm room (tepidarium) where they stayed a while before entering a hot room (caldarium). Sweating from the heat cleansed the pores, and the sweat could be wiped off using a strigil (a scraping implement) or by washing in a hot bath. Then the bathers returned to the warm room before proceeding into a cold room (frigidarium) and entered a cold plunge bath. Finally, they returned to the undressing room to be dried, oiled and dressed.*

room (perhaps the estate office) and front, northern and rear corridors. The latter was divided into two rooms, the southern probably being a kitchen. Occupying the building's western end a bath suite consisted of an access corridor, cold room, cold plunge bath, hot plunge bath, hot and warm rooms, an internal furnace room that fired the hypocausts, and there was a southern wing room probably functioning as an undressing room. Taking all rooms into account they are clearly insufficient to accommodate the needs of a family. This lack of ground floor rooms argues very strongly for a multi-storey building, if only in its central core. Over the next century several changes were made within the house. Fired from the adjacent bath suite's furnace room, a circular

*Fig. 18. Villa House Remains*

channelled hypocaust was inserted into the central room. Reduction of the furnace room and the bath's access corridor enabled the insertion of a dry heat room. A slightly larger cold plunge bath replaced the former while a larger kitchen was constructed over the site of the old. Elements within the latter included a cooking range, an oven, a tripod stand and a sand trough. Of particular importance relating to the variety of food prepared and consumed is the house's new kitchen layout and sealed deposits within it and to its exterior. The room's initial clay floor was replaced many times either in gravel, sand, clay, mortar, or concrete. Between the various floor layers of ash, some quite thick, were found a variety of food items such as spelt wheat grain, fish and chicken bones, and eggshells. Waste deposits dumped outside the kitchen during the latter part of the second/early third centuries contained similar remains plus animal bones, mollusc shells, much pottery, and window and glass vessel fragments. Identification of the animal bone reveals that there was only a slight change from the farmhouse phase in the animals consumed, as there was only a small drop in the total of cattle bones, a minor rise in the number of sheep/goat bones, whilst the amount of pig bones remained the same.

*Fig. 19. Villa house kitchen*

Evident wealth was displayed in the embellishment of the house since, while no tessellated or mosaic paving survived, it is clear from the numerous loose tesserae found, and the waste from their manufacture, that they had existed. Also indicating the owner's prosperity, fragments of painted wall plaster were discovered depicting bordered panels with floral and vegetal designs, architecture, figures, fish, and marbling, all in a range of colours – mainly red, green, blue, and black.

Contemporary with the house and erected close to its rear a 4.9-metres by 6.1-metres single-roomed structure contained a central hearth. Screened by the house from the courtyard this building would have probably served as accommodation for some of the house servants. A similarly located building is evident on the Roman villa at Brading on the Isle of Wight (Cunliffe 2013).

On the southern side of the house a flint-block lined well had been dug to supply the bath suite, kitchen, household, and gardens with water.

Fig. 20. Villa well

Further to the south an east to west boundary ditch divided the courtyard area from farmland. Subsequently erected over this a 12.25-metres by 25-metres barn had a wide entrance on its southern side that gave direct access to the fields without the need to enter the courtyard. Inside, close to the north wall, lay a row of eight equidistant post pads. These presumably supported stalling for animals, most likely oxen. If this is the case seven stalls are present each being 3-metres wide and 2.5-metres-long. This is close to the 3-metres by 2.7-metres suggested by Vitruvius (a first century BC author) for the keeping of oxen (Morris 1979). Ox was the main draught animal and they needed stalling to control their diet and to provide protection and convenience. The remainder of the building could have been used for the storage of wagons, carts, ploughs, and harness etc., and perhaps in a loft, animal feed and hay. Later, a single-roomed structure was added to the building's western end.

Between the barn and the house, a small 2.5-metres square structure had been pre-dated by a rectilinear pit of unknown function. Indicating that the structure had an important purpose is its isolated location and later embellishment with a new façade. Comparison can be made with a small isolated and internally apsed structure set into the courtyard wall at Brading Roman villa, where it has been identified as a water shrine (*nymphaeum*).

West of the barn a rectangular 7.5-metres by 9-metres building located in the villa courtyard's south-east corner replaced an earlier stone structure of which little trace remained. The presence in the new building of an internal drain that discharged into a large external pit, and its location close to the courtyard entrance, suggest strongly that the structure was used for stabling animals, probably horses. An internal post pad's position indicates two stalls identical in size to the envisaged ox stalls seen in the southern barn. Externally a line of substantial post pits show that a boundary fence extended from the building's north-east corner towards the road.

Fig. 21. Drier foundations c. AD 180

Following the demolition of the internal features the riverside building was extended to 28-metres-long and re-floored with chalk. Four sheep had been slaughtered and buried in two pits beneath the floor as offerings to the relevant deities, so ensuring continued prosperity. They also may indicate the presence and importance of sheep-rearing to the farming estate at that time. Refurbished, the building now incorporated at its western end a new drier that had curved heating channels, a centrally located oven, a stone slab-floored tank, a tiny T-shaped drier and possibly a slave mill defined by a worn circular groove in the chalk floor. At the eastern end, a very large timber tank connected with the road's drainage ditch via a short channel. Making the building accessible to carts a substantial timber bridge now existed, its oak foundation beams surviving at the bottom of the road's drainage ditch. Sealed inside the floor's make-up a worn coin (*sestertius*) of the Emperor Hadrian (AD 117 to 138) dated the re-vamp to the mid or latter half of the second century. The new drier now had two individually fired heating channels which would have enabled drying of smaller quantities of goods without heating the whole structure. During its life the drier was renovated at least once as the channelling was altered. Based on the size of the new timber tank, it appears that manufacture of malt/beer continued at a much larger scale, implying a ready market. Medieval brewing records indicate that full use of the 3.2-metres wide, 3.4-metres-long tank could potentially result in 1,500 gallons of very strong ale being produced every ten to twelve days using fourteen quarters of barley. Large scale bread production hinted at in the building's earlier phase must have ceased as only a single terracotta tile-walled oven was now present.

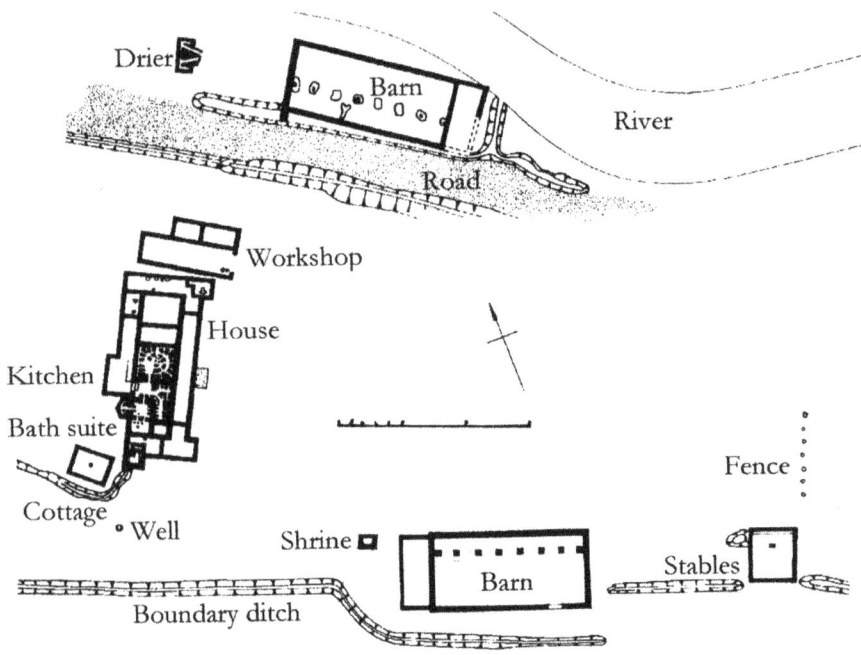

*Fig. 22. Villa complex c. AD 230*

Besides numerous quern-stone fragments recovered from the building and the adjacent road ditch fill from the nearby riverbed came half of a large millstone. Cereal remains from deposits within or adjacent to the building include barley, emmer, and hulled wheat – chiefly spelt. Evidence of germination of hulled wheat in the timber tank and the drier confirmed the continued malting process. Barley and oat grains recovered from the north road ditch silt adjacent to the building also showed traces of germination.

If the riverside building served as a wayside tavern that function ceased at the beginning of, or early in the third century AD when levelling of the building occurred. It is possible that this was due to the road having been rerouted, as a Roman road has been recently traced and settlement evidence beneath Chilton Foliat found on the opposite side of the river. Encroaching over part of the riverside building's demolished remains a flint-walled barn was then erected, its dimensions being 11.8-metres by 24.7-metres. This may point to a change in the villa's farming practices and source of income, although the retention of the drier shows that corn was still grown. The fact that the new barn's roof ridge, supported by post pads, was clearly off-centre is unusual. Perhaps such an arrangement permitted ease of access to or created more roof storage space. Another odd feature is the western end wall being, at 1.1-metres, much thicker than the other walls, and it was heavily buttressed at its southern end. Perhaps it supported an upper feature such as a bell tower. Within the building two sheep carcases were buried prior to the laying of a chalk floor, demonstrating the continued ritual performed as an act of offering to the gods. The function of the building is obscure other than partly as a blacksmith's smithy. A sequence of a bowl furnace followed by a shaft furnace and the need for repair of the chalk floor suggests that this may have been

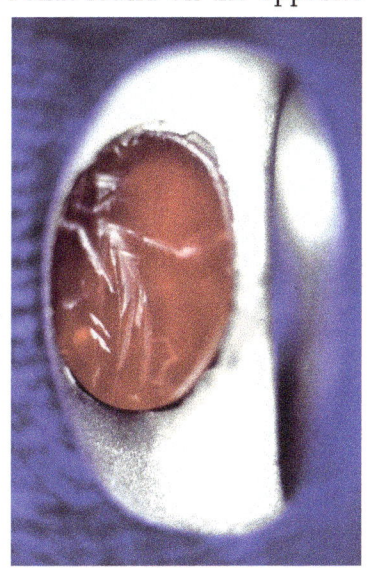

Fig. 23. Silver ring set with an intaglio depicting the god Sol from Littlecote

for a fairly long period of time. Clearly the manufacture from iron ore of farming equipment and the repair of such took place. The remainder of the barn was, most likely, used for crop and equipment storage. Subsequently a single room was added at the eastern end that could have provided accommodation for workers.

Several artefacts recovered during this phase tell of the religious convictions of the inhabitants. Three pipe clay figurine fragments, including part of a *Dea Nutrix* (nursing mother figure), certainly came from a household shrine, as did also a fragment from a bronze figurine. Two ring intaglios also portray deities. A carnelian set in a silver ring depicts *Sol,* who was the solar deity, and a carnelian found in a ploughed field overlooking the site shows *Victoria* crowning *Fortuna,* the goddess of fortune and essence of luck, good or bad, in Roman religion. A small bronze bell found near the river may also have a religious connotation. Christianity is represented by a pottery black-burnished ware platter that is internally incised with a *Chi-Rho* (the first two letters of Christ's name, being in Greek – ΧΡΙΣΤΟΣ) and may have been used in serving communion amongst the estate workers.

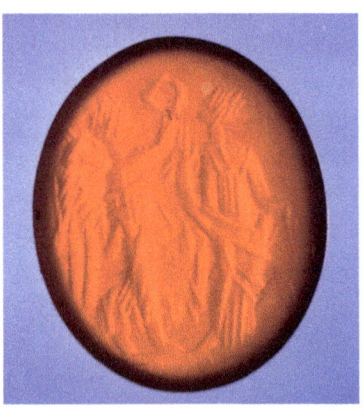

Fig. 24. Carnelian intaglio from Littlecote depicting Victoria crowning Fortuna

As wealth accumulated through the sale of the surplus agricultural produce to the military and civilian markets, the owner was able to erect new buildings, embellish existing structures and purchase the services and luxury goods provided by the Roman world. Notable amongst the latter and displaying the potential wealth are finds of a gold earring fragment and a silver spoon. Scratched in the bowl of the spoon are the letters CVP, presumably, an abbreviation of its owner's name. Also, there are fine pottery vessels and quality glass vessels (bowls, bottles, cups, beakers, jars, jugs, and flasks) such as might be expected on a well-to-do villa site. Amongst the imported fine pottery wares was an increased amount of Samian ware (including decorated) as well as black-slipped ware from the Trier area and Central Gaulish black-slipped ware. The desire for British fine wares was also

*Fig. 25. Bronze smelting furnace in the villa house*

clearly coming to the fore with North Wiltshire colour-coated beakers and Nene Valley colour-coated wares being present. Marked amphorae indicate that olive oil came from southern Spain and wine came from Gaul. It is of note that two flagon sherds from the kitchen midden were incised with small numerals VIII (8) and XII (12) which perhaps signify a way of recording their content – most probably varieties of wine.

This constructional phase terminated with a burst of short-lived industrial activity dated by sealed coins to the latter half of the third century AD. Small-scale smelting of scrap copper alloy items took place in the workshop and strangely inside the house's rear corridor, north corridor, and north wing room. This activity involved the construction of small charcoal and coal-fuelled crucible furnaces: two in the house and three in the workshop. In the workshop the furnaces were not contemporary but were constructed one after the other on the same spot close to the building's eastern entrance. The furnaces took the form of an inverted T-cutting with the shaft forming the base of the furnace area and the crossbar the lighting/ash removal channel, and which almost certainly gave access for bellows. The shafts had straight sides lined in one example and probably all originally with large thin stone slabs. On the flat furnace bases traces of burning were apparent, overlain in most cases by ash. From the north wing room furnace came small scraps of bronze sheets and bronze slag, whilst the final workshop furnace contained coal lumps, coal dust and finely crushed terracotta tile fragments. The latter was also present in the house's north wing room furnace and piled against the south wall of the north corridor. Evidently crushed tile performed some function in the industrial process, perhaps in mould or crucible manufacture. Also found in the corridor against the walls were two areas of burning and a shallow 6-centimetres deep and 0.45-metre by 0.49-metre rectangular depression which had angled sides and a flat bottom, and which contained a light spread of coal fragments. Adjacent were smallish coal fragments spread over an area 0.25-metre-wide and 1.1-metres-long. It is feasible that the hollow represented an anvil location and the coal residue of lumps that had been broken up on it. Coal is an uncommon commodity on Roman sites. Scientific analysis has shown that the Littlecote coal had been mined on the Avon and Somerset coalfield (Smith 1997). Whether this industrial process implies a decline in the estate fortunes or covert activity by the estate owner is unclear. This event, however, was taking place at a time when counterfeiting of coins was prevalent. Is this the situation at Littlecote? Similar activity has been noted on several other villa sites in the region (i.e., Frocester Court in Gloucestershire and North Leigh in Oxfordshire). Seemingly the villa-owning aristocracy had discovered a way to supplement their wealth.

# 8
# Villa Courtyard Complex (AD 300-360)

Following the covert industrial activity of the previous constructional phase a major re-development of the entire courtyard complex seems to have been triggered by a sudden increase in prosperity. What caused this event can only be surmised, perhaps the property had passed into new hands, or it was an investment by the original family based on wealth accrued. The alterations to the house one hundred years after its erection were extensive, in fact almost a complete rebuild. As part of these alterations the house underwent partial demolition. The front corridor, wing rooms, cold room, cold plunge bath, hot bath, and kitchen, and at least partly the north and rear corridors were levelled leaving

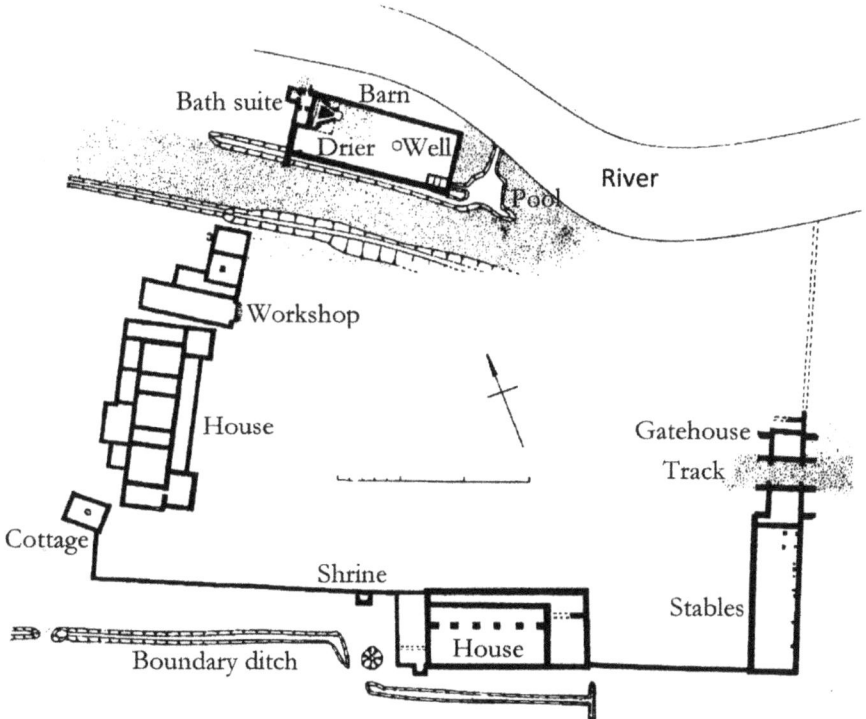

*Fig. 26. Villa complex c. AD 300*

*Fig. 27. Villa house AD 360*

only the outer shell of the central core standing. The most dramatic architectural change was to the replacement wing rooms that now had substantial foundations and which, undoubtedly, comprised at least two and perhaps three stories. Certainly, the southern wing room had replaced the formerly heated central room as the principal reception/dining room, for it now incorporated the sole hypocaust within the rebuilt house. Its furnace lay within a room constructed over the former cold room/cold plunge which based on its size could also have served as a wood store. Internal access from or to the rebuilt kitchen was now achieved via a corridor constructed over the former furnace room or along the rear corridor. A small room added to the new kitchen above the former hot plunge bath may have served as a store or access to a large unheated room constructed over the previous baths hot and cold rooms, their access corridor, and part of the dry heat room. Most of the main rooms and the front corridor were clearly embellished with mosaics,

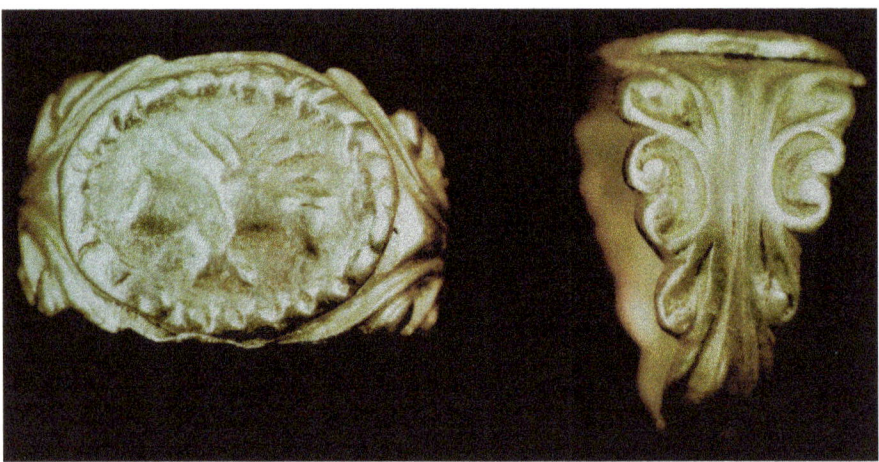

*Fig. 28. Gold betrothal ring found in the villa house*

although due to later medieval activity little trace remained apart from a few patches of tessellated borders and flooring. From the floor bedding of the central block's northern room came a third-century gold betrothal ring that depicts clasped hands. One wonders what story lies behind its loss. The walls of the north and rear corridors which had been partially or wholly demolished were then rebuilt on their original foundations. The rear and northern corridors, in stark contrast to the grandeur of the other rooms, received floors made up of builders' debris (mosaic manufacture waste and painted wall plaster stripped from walls of the former house) clearly demonstrating their lesser status, being primarily used by servants.

Extending northwards from the workers cottage at the rear of the villa house a courtyard wall was erected to provide privacy and security. Turning east and crossing the now infilled well it linked with the front of the garden shrine. From the shrine's opposite side the wall continued to join the front of the southern barn's extension. At the opposite end of the barn close to its rear a further stretch linked with the stable block's south-west corner. South of the house near to the south-west corner of this courtyard wall a foundation pad was placed which was probably part of a garden shelter/arbour. Indeed, it is feasible that this area between the courtyard wall and the south end of the house had become a formal garden, as hinted at by areas of paving and a build-up of loam, unfortunately much disturbed in the medieval period.

Alterations to the barn on the courtyard's south side apparently changed its function, at least in part, to residential. Demonstrating this a corridor now linked the building's western extension to two newly formed rooms at the building's eastern end and fronted a freshly created large work-hall to its rear, whilst the former wide southern entrance was blocked. The insertion of six substantial ridge support post pads within the hall show that the changes had included restructuring and then re- tiling of the roof. Converting the bath suite in the house into accommodation had meant that the villa now lacked bathing facilities. However, it is likely that this was the time when the western extension to the south barn was undergoing conversion to a bath suite. For reasons unknown, despite the partial demolition and re-building of the exterior walling, including insertion of wall flue tiles and an apsidal hot bath, the interior building work was never completed and neither a stoke pit dug nor a firing flue inserted. Just outside the building digging of a huge pit for the construction of a well had commenced, but it was never finished.

Demolition of the stable block in the courtyard's south-west corner occurred enabling the erection of a 7-metres wide and 23.5-metres-long rectangular single-roomed building. Internal post pits and stone post pads indicate the presence of stalling for horses and perhaps oxen. The building's 1.04-metres-deep foundations indicate two stories, the uppermost probably served for staff lodging and storage. Adjoining the building's south-west corner and extending westward, set further back from, and replacing the former courtyard wall that had suffered from subsidence, a new boundary wall had been erected. A further freestanding wall was built extending north from the stable block's north-east corner towards the road. Later, the foundation for an elaborate gateway was inserted within it. This shows that the presumed courtyard entrance on the former military road had been blocked, access now being diverted a short distance to the south to provide a direct approach to the villa house. Eventually, replacing the gateway and adjoining the stable block, a dramatic gatehouse was erected for which the ground floor plan took the form of two buttressed rooms separated by an arched passageway. Overall, this structure measured 9-metres by 13.5-metres with the passageway being 4-metres wide and the foundations up to 0.86-metre deep. This entrance to the villa courtyard must rank high amongst the most flamboyant on any villa site in Britain. Its plan is very reminiscent of a military granary apart from the presence of the central passage, and is comparable in size to a

*Fig. 29. The gatehouse foundations*

*Fig. 30. The villa gatehouse reconstruction*

granary at Chesters fort on Hadrian's Wall (Gentry 1976). In granaries buttresses were required to withstand the outward thrust of stored grain and substantial foundations withstood vertical pressure. The presence of these on the Littlecote gatehouse makes it highly feasible that an upper floor was for storage of grain. The principal features of a granary were to reduce moisture content and temperature to prevent mould, bacterial and fungal growth, and to minimise the activity of insects and rodents. Being on an upper floor it would have served, with adequate ventilation, that purpose. Adding to the possibility of a granary, fronting the building's southern tower were traces of a sequence of paving which eventually became a large, raised platform. These could have facilitated the loading and unloading of carts with grain sacks, animal fodder or hay. From the platform sacks could have been hoisted into or lowered from an upper floor. Extending from the east of the gatehouse and passing through the passageway into the courtyard was a sequence of track surfaces. These underwent many repairs and periods of silting, evidencing much use over a long period of time. The presence of a freestanding wall followed by the erection of a building were revealed on the gatehouse's northern side by chalk foundations. Regrettably, these had been largely destroyed by the cutting of a very extensive hollow during the medieval period.

Demolition of the riverside barn's front wall occurred, and it was rebuilt further back apparently to aid the removal of the interior roof support columns and so create

Fig. 31. Riverside barn

a single-span stone-tiled roof set over an open chalk-floored interior. In the building's north-west corner a small bath suite was erected. Comprising hot and warm rooms and a hot plunge bath, its hypocausts were fired via a flue constructed in the barn's riverside wall. Entrance to the baths was from the building's interior, suggesting that it was intended for the villa workers' use.

Abutting the bath suite's eastern wall, a double flue drier was built like the one west of the barn. A little to the east of the barn's drier a packed flint-block and chalk floored area was superimposed on the building's chalk floor. Central to the barn a 1.56-metres-deep well was revealed. In the south-east corner a 1.7-metres-wide, 3.55-metres-long, 0.5-metre-deep wooden tank survived as timber impressions with iron nails embedded in the pit's clay lining. Slots in the pit's floor show that it was divided into three equal compartments by moveable screens. From the tank a drain passed through the barn's eastern wall into a large pool that was linked to the road's northern drainage ditch, and this was joined to the river by another ditch. Surrounding the pool and lining, and flooring it, was a thick gravel layer.

Eventually the drier was demolished to make-way for an extended bath suite that included a mortar-floored dressing room and cold room; the latter had a cold plunge bath. In the dressing room a fireplace set partly into a niche cut into the south wall had as a base a large flat sarsen stone. Adjacent wide steps gave access to the road. It may have been that the lack of a bath suite within the house following its renovation and the failure to complete the construction of the bath suite in the south barn was resolved by the now extended bath suite. Its use therefore reverted from workers to the villa owner and his family.

The barn's other internal features provide evidence along with the stables of farming activity during this phase at Littlecote and this is amongst the most graphic for a villa site in Roman Britain. Within the barn the various elements reveal the variety of the estate's produce and some of the methods of processing it, notably wool and grain production. The double T-shaped drier could have been a replacement for the comparable drier located west of the barn which been retained following the demolition of the malt house, or an extra one due to an increase in grain production. Lying to the rear of the drier's stoke pits the extensive flint-block- and chalk-packed floor may have been a threshing floor or hard standing for carts which brought the produce in to be dried. An eight-centimetres-deep layer of fuller's earth remaining on the base of the tank in the barn's south-east corner demonstrates that it functioned as a cleansing tank for sheep fleeces. The divisions indicated within it probably represented separate compartments for various stages in the cleansing process. This involved treading fleeces in a mixture of fuller's earth that served to scour out grease and dirt, followed by rinsing in the river to remove any remaining fuller's earth.

*The woollen industry played a significant part in the wealth of Roman Britain as highlighted by the 'Edict of Diocletian' in AD 301 – a conspectus of traded goods and services available across the Empire. The British birrus, a woollen hooded cloak, ranked sixth whilst the tapete, a woollen rug, came first on another list (Wild 2002).*

After this it is likely that the wool was hung out to dry and then bundled up ready for transporting to market. Some would have been retained for spinning into yarn for the inhabitants' own use, as demonstrated by the finding of spindle whorls – weights used with a spindle to draw thread from wool. The centrally-located well would have supplied the cleansing pit and the initial bath suite. However, the large pool into which the cleansing tank drained, and which had a gravelled floor and sides, may well have served as a watering hole for animals, particularly sheep brought in for shearing. Notably the consumption of mutton, shown by the animal bones recovered, fell greatly during this phase from 56% to 31% whilst the eating of beef increased from 31% to 67%. Rather than being a reduction in sheep rearing, this is indicative of sheep being kept for their wool rather than their meat. From silt in the well and the road drainage ditch fronting the building came carbonised wheat grain, clearly derived from activities within the barn. Germinated grains found among them imply malt production and perhaps another function for the wooden tank – steeping grain.

Accidental coin loss during this phase fell after the third quarter of the third century but remained relatively high. Then, following regional trends, it rose sharply for the second quarter of the fourth century (Moorhead 2001).

British fine ware pottery had now become dominant over imports, filling the gap in the market left by a decline in the Samian ware industry. This can be seen in the vessels sourced by the villa inhabitants. From the Oxfordshire kilns came red-coated dishes and bowls, whilst the New Forest kilns provided beakers and some bowls, jugs, flagons, and jars.

# 9
# Orphic Complex (AD 360-65)

Alterations and embellishment of this phase c. AD 360, saw the transformation of the courtyard structures to a complex designed for a specific purpose, being either ritual or as an extravagant display by a wealthy landowner. This included removal of all traces of agricultural activity from in and around the courtyard.

Fronting the heated south wing room of the house a substantial foundation for a superficial façade slightly overlapped the room's frontage at its southern end. At the other end it incorporated a short pier, adjoining which and extending parallel to the house frontage lay a slight 4.85 metres long flint-block foundation, most likely the footing for a timber sill beam that supported a flight of timber steps. At its northern

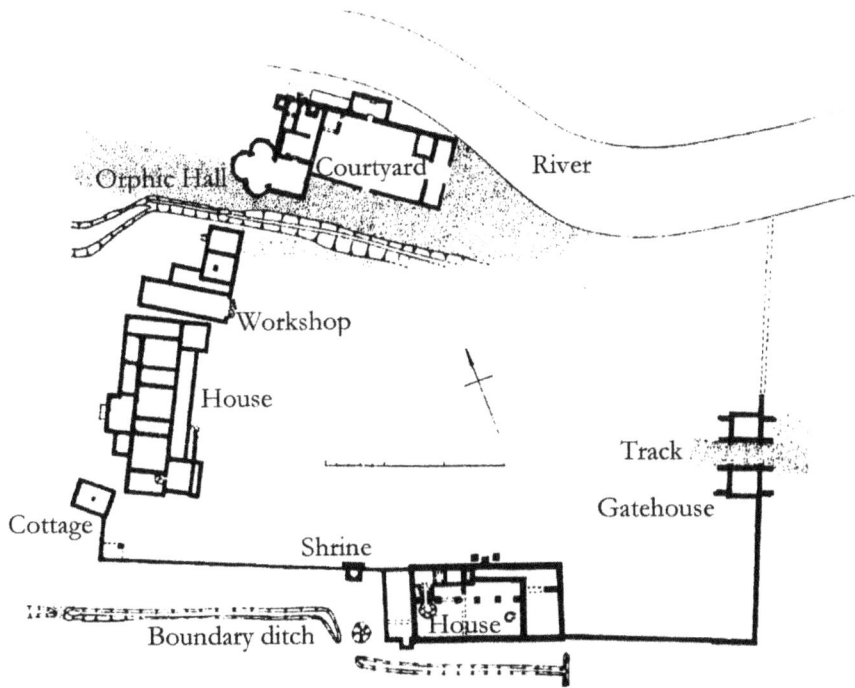

*Fig. 32. Orphic complex c. AD 365*

end, extending to the house's corridor wall, a rectangular area of flint packing probably represented a base for a stone step. In the light of this apparent stairway that fronted the building's corridor the new façade may have incorporated a balcony at a higher level. Similarly, the likely garden shrine was fronted by a compacted chalk foundation implying that it, correspondingly, had received a new façade, perhaps columned. Not to be outdone, the southern building shown by chalk foundation pads was centrally adorned with a columned porch and steps. Also, within the building a bath suite was inserted into the corridor's western end and partly extending into the work hall, where a stoke pit for firing its hypocausts was dug. The suite comprised a hot room, a hot bath, a warm room, a cold room, a cold plunge bath, and a dressing room, although only slight traces of the latter's walling remained. The hot and warm room floors had been supported on terracotta *pilae* tile stacks. Water drained from the cold plunge via a lead pipe that was still set in the fillet of the *opus signinum* floor; this emerged out of the building into a stone-lined and capped drain set into the courtyard. Furthermore, around this time the apparent levelling of the buildings flanking the gatehouse occurred while, feasibly, the preservation of the east walls, reduced in height, kept the enclosed courtyard concept.

*Fig. 33. The riverside Orphic building*

*Fig. 34. Orpheus mosaic following relaying and restoration, completed 1980*

The greatest and most dramatic changes were reserved for the riverside barn. Firstly, a triple-apsed hall was added to the south-west corner. Inside the room a mosaic was laid. A wall had been erected within the barn's bath suite dressing room (*apodyterium*), its foundation trench cutting through the eastern edge of the entrance steps that had given access to and from the road, but now served the hall. It created a corridor that provided access to the bath suite without the need to enter the former dressing room, a room now definable as the hall's anteroom. A coin of Constans found in the wall's foundation trench backfill dates to AD 345-8. During this phase, or the next, the fireplace in the room was altered to incorporate an oven. Within the frigidarium, against its south wall, a well packed layer of small flint-blocks, most likely bedding for a new floor, had been laid down. Filling the gaps between the stones

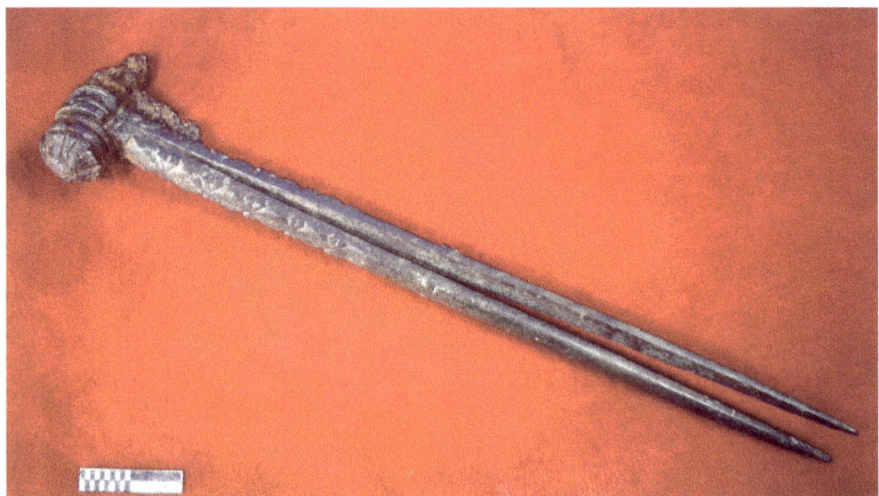

*Fig. 35. Bronze dividers from the Orphic building*

and forming an overlying deposit, mosaic manufacture waste comprised numerous stone and terracotta tile chippings. Also, from between the stones came a coin of the house of Constantine, also datable to AD 345-8. The barn's former agricultural area had now been largely demolished, leaving only the bath suite at its west end and with the barn's rear wall and east wall being reduced in height. Rebuilt, a now free-standing front wall incorporated four equally spaced niches, set above sarsen foundation pads which would have supported stone columns. Behind the wall and open to the elements, now lay a 10.6-metres by 19-metres stone slab paved courtyard. From the floor's mortar bedding came a coin of Constans minted c. AD 337-341. Erected in the north-east corner a small room conceivably served as a temporary workshop for mosaic cube manufacture. Piles of waste from their cutting lay on its floor and more were packed into its foundation trench along with an *Urbs Roma* coin of AD 330-337. In the courtyard's mortar bedding an oval-shaped depression had been reddened by heat. Later above this a room like that in the north-east corner had been erected and floored in mortar. Sealed in the floor were three bronze coins – a Constantinian copy c. AD 335-345, a coin of Constantius II AD 337 to 361 and a coin of Constans c. AD 337 to 350. Attached externally at the eastern end of the courtyard an 11.8-metres by 3.4-metres mortar floored rectangular room possibly

*Fig. 36. Orpheus on the mosaic*

served as *narthex* (entrance hall). It had a wide east-facing doorway, which gave a clear downstream view of the river. It may have been contemporary with the initial construction or a little later. Immediately to the rear of and accessed from the courtyard, a further room was added. From its mortar floor came a pair of decorated bronze dividers of late fourth century date. Abutting its west wall and that of the former barn, a 1.8-metres-wide and 6.24-metres-long rectangular flint and mortar raft most likely served as the base for a large water tank built to supply the extended bath suite. The largely silted-up watering hole just a little to the east of the building had been, or was at this time, infilled with flint-blocks and overlaid with a packed flint gravel and clay yard. River silt overlying it contained a coin of Constantius II c. AD 337-361.

Clearly the focus of this constructional phase was the riverside building with its triple-apsed hall, unique in Romano-British architecture, which is also remarkably early when compared to similar structures in the Roman Empire. It seems that the Littlecote owner and the architect had concepts in mind when they planned the building. In some ways though it seems they were adding to the design as it was under construction rather than a singular planned build. First the triple-apsed hall seems to have been added, then the walled courtyard with its elaborate columned frontage, next small rooms in the north-eastern and north-western corners, a room to the courtyard's rear and finally the entrance hall with its view along the river.

The mosaic laid within the hall, when uncovered in 1978, was found to have only partly survived, but it was fully restored using the eighteenth-century engraving made in 1727 when it must have been almost entirely intact. The mosaic's Orphic imagery has abundant art-historical significance. Its imagery combines *Orpheus* with *Apollo* and *Bacchus*. Depicted at its centre *Orpheus* plays a lyre, at his side there is a leaping dog and surrounding him is a circle of four animals – a goat, a panther, a bull, and a deer – and four dancing females distinguishable by their attributes as goddesses – *Persephone, Venus, Nemesis* or *Leda*, and *Demeter*. In the apses panther heads radiate light, whilst a stylised pool divides the apsed end from the hall. In the latter two leopards paw at a wine crater, four lotus flower heads are surrounded by a Greek key design and sea beasts face another wine crater, whilst dolphins swim away, all enclosed by a chequered border. These images relate to the cycle of life, the seasons, rebirth, and mythology relating to the Greek God *Dionysus* (*Bacchus* in the Roman world) and his priest *Orpheus*. It is possible the mosaic has links to the Corinium School of mosaicists, which appears to have specialised in Orphic pavements. *Orpheus* in the Roman world was the prophet of *Bacchus* the God of the grape harvest, winemaking, wine, and of ritual madness and ecstasy.

Demonstrating the on-site manufacture of the *Orpheus* mosaic is the large quantity of raw material (150.065kg) found dumped in and around the building – hard chalk blocks, waste from cutting chalk blocks, terracotta and stone tiles cut into tesserae. Included are small, formed sticks of stone ready for cutting into mosaic tesserae and a large limestone 'rubber' for smoothing tessellated floor surfaces. These deposits provide a useful insight into the working practices of itinerate craftsmen manufacturing mosaics on-site.

Several artefacts recovered also indicate the owner's Bacchic beliefs. From the building's rear room came a large part of a 'face-pot' wine crater moulded with grape and panther motifs. This was made at a pottery at Much Hadham in Hertfordshire (Braithwaite 1984). Most telling though are two bronze chest fittings found together in

*Fig. 37. Busts of Bacchus and Antinous from Littlecote*

plough soil on the hill overlooking the complex. These are a small bust of *Bacchus* and another of *Bacchus-Antinous* (Henig 1988). Deified in October AD 130 following his death by drowning in the Nile, Antinous, the favourite courtier of the Emperor Hadrian, became identified with *Zagreus-Bacchus* in the late empire. Dated to the second or third quarter of the second century these bronzes would have been heirlooms at the time of the Orphic Hall construction.

The unusual layout, its isolation from other structures and the iconography presented on the mosaic has led to much speculation as to the function of the structure. Was it a complex designed for ritual or pleasure? Walters has put forward the idea that the site had now passed into the hands of a Bacchic cult (Walters 1984), a suggestion that fits in well with the lack of agricultural traces, the alterations to existing structures, finds, date, and iconographic evidence. Then the hall would have served for ceremonial and philosophical meetings for a select elite and, as bathing and feasting formed part of the Bacchic ritual, the presence of the bath-suite presents no problems. The oblong panels in the south and north apses contain two rows of linked circles seemingly at odds with the rest of the design. Perhaps these present the location for benches or chairs. The chequered border in the hall could be the location for further benches. Clearly the mosaic imagery was meant to be viewed from the top apse, apart from the sea beast and dolphin panel which had to be viewed from the hall's eastern end. The mysteries of his cult were closely guarded, hence the apparent need for a secluded complex set in the countryside. The entrance hall could have been a gathering place or waiting area prior to crossing the courtyard to take part in ceremonies in the Orphic Hall.

It is of note that most of the coins lost at Littlecote at this time were found in and around the riverside barn during its conversion. This implies low value monetary transactions were taking place, perhaps gambling by the builders during rest periods. Apart from one of Allectus, all are of the Constantinian dynasty, with half being from the reigns of Constans AD 337-350 and Constantius II AD 337-361. Allowing for time to circulate and wear it is conceivable that the conversion of the building took place during the reign of Julian (AD 360-3). Julian attempted to revive traditional religious practices at the cost of Christianity. His rejection of Christianity in favour of neoplatonic paganism caused him

ARCHAEOLOGICAL EXCAVATIONS IN THE PARK 47

Fig. 38. Interior of the Orphic Hall

to be known as Julian the Apostate. Perhaps this revival is shown in the creation of the complex at Littlecote.

On the other hand, the Bacchic evidence may be only an expression of the owner's personal beliefs. *Bacchus* was worshipped in celebration of the powers of nature by feasting, drinking, music, and dance, apt for a wealthy country estate owner. Those beliefs must have been extraordinarily strong for the owner to build this unique architectural structure floored with a mosaic displaying complex Bacchic imagery. In this case the complex could be seen as an elaborate retreat that included a dining room, bath suite and exercise courtyard on the riverside as suggested by Ellis (Ellis 1995). Cosh (Cosh 2001) believes it is not an exotic summer dining room as it lacks a kitchen, and suggests it is instead an elaborate room associated with bathing. Though perhaps Cosh would agree if he noted that the anteroom had at some point had an oven/cooking range inserted. Witts (Witts 2000) on the other hand points out that the size of the apses is insufficient to take dining couches which would require apses at least 4-metres to 5-metres-wide and 2-metres to 2.5-metres-deep. The Littlecote apses are for the southern 2.2-metres by 3.4-metres the western 2.5-metres by 3.6-metres and the northern 2.6-metres by 3.4-metres.

Such a complex, whether the owner's display of his wealth, or an establishment for a religious cult, would have required substantial financial input to build and maintain it. It may be that for the former, due to the owner's desire to be secluded from the sights, smells, and sounds of the farm, the agricultural function had been removed to an area further to the east or, if a cult centre, funds were provided by wealthy exponents.

## 10
# Decline and Decay (AD 365-450)

Following the construction of the Orphic complex there are few signs of building activity, and what there is appears minor suggesting a period of stagnation or the commencement of a decline in the complex's fortunes. The work that was done appears to have been the conversion of the riverside building into a house, as two rooms were added to the courtyard's rear; the conversion of the fireplace in the hall's anteroom into an oven/cooking range may have taken place at this time. An oven was inserted within the southern building's hall and a cooking pit was cut into

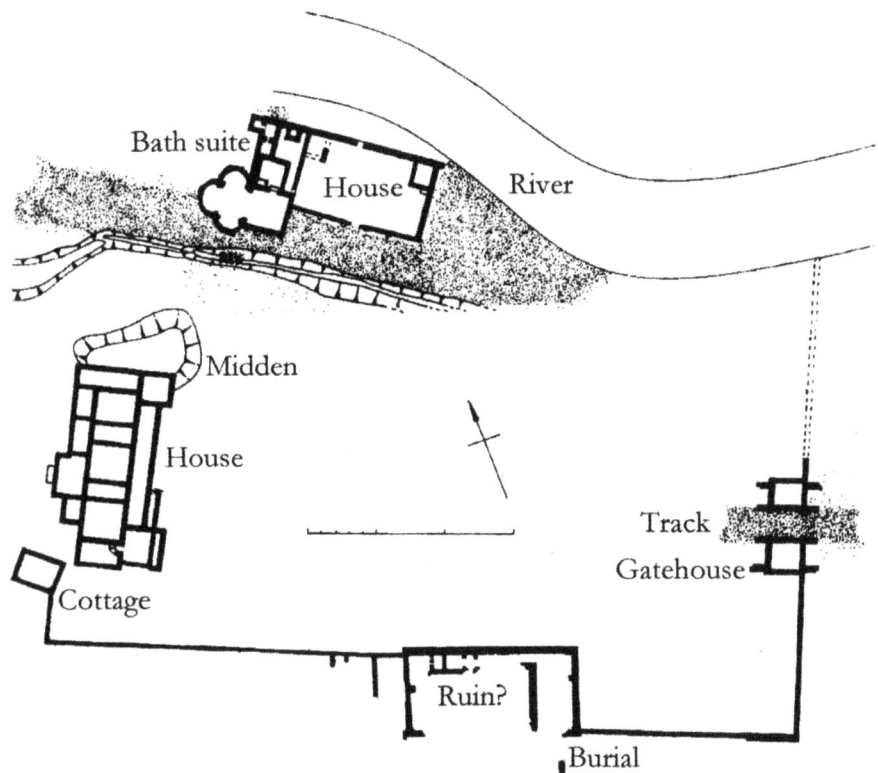

*Fig. 39. Villa c. AD 420*

the fill of the boundary ditch at the building's rear. Consequently, the complex now apparently consisted of four dwellings: the southern and northern buildings, the workshop, and its domestic wing, and the villa house. Self-contained, multiple, tenancy on villa sites in the late Roman period has been noted elsewhere. Of further note at this time, indicated by post pits, the gatehouse passage was provided with an outer gate.

A study (Moorhead 2001) of the coins from 44 sites in Wiltshire showed a high number of Valentinianic bronze coins (AD 364-378). Moorhead believes this outlines the regions where food and other natural resources were being exploited for the *annona militaris* (an unofficial tax in kind) by the Roman authorities for export to the Continent, notably the Rhineland. Indeed, it is quite likely that the late fortified Roman town of *Cvnetio* (Mildenhall), lying on the southern bank of the River Kennet, a short distance upstream from Littlecote, was a local collection centre. Here exploited food and other natural resources could have been gathered and stored prior to shipment. Then these goods might easily have been shipped on the river downstream to *Londinium* (London) and beyond. At Littlecote though coin loss was now low, perhaps signifying decline or the lack of monetary transactions. Coin loss then increases in the late fourth century with bronze coins of Arcadius issued AD 383 to AD 402, and Honorius issued AD 393 to AD 402. These were distributed in the vicinity of the workshop and to the south of the house with a slight scatter by the house, the southern building, and the gatehouse. High numbers of late Roman coin loss is a feature that has been identified in the region, a trait particularly noted on the small towns and roadside settlements with, strangely, at this time the exception of *Cvnetio* (Moorhead 2001).

Animal consumption on the site now comprised almost entirely cattle 91% with a few sheep/goats 5% and pigs 4%. Clearly indicated is a change not only in diet but probably in farming practices, that once again promoted a rise in monetary transactions and presumably some wealth.

Obvious signs of decay were soon indicated by accumulations of collapse and destruction debris – flint-blocks, stone roofing tiles, mortar, terracotta tiles, tesserae, wall plaster and tufa. Whilst these were gathering, clear signs of occupation were still evident in the winged house and the courtyard's north and south buildings. However, the workshop and its wing had collapsed with its debris overlying the building and extending in front of the house's northern end. From this debris came a coin of Honorius issued between AD 395 and AD 402. The northern side wall of the workshop's western part, originally the smokehouse, fell intact. White sandstone slabs on the uppermost course may represent roof plates showing that it had stood to a height of around six-metres. Over this and adjacent debris an extensive kitchen midden slowly accumulated that contained a large amount of late Roman pottery, glassware, oyster shell, and animal bone.

Fig. 40. Building demolition debris in the south building's bath house stoke pit

In the mid to late fifth century, building debris from the house decay or collapse overlay the midden as well as the north corridor of the house, the rear corridor rooms, and extended onto the building's backyard. In the Orphic complex the various rooms of the bath suite, the ante room to the hall, the courtyard, and the courtyard's north-eastern room gradually accumulated a mixture of loam and mortar which resulted from the decay and disturbance of underlying mortar flooring/bedding. Over this, in the eastern part of the courtyard, levelled destruction debris lay up to 0.4-metre-high. Yet in this and adjacent to the courtyard's north-east corner room a rectangular 1.3-metres by 1.68-metres flint-block construction was defined. The surrounding debris was well packed down with the surface stones being rounded and chipped, unlike debris elsewhere, which suggested that the feature, perhaps the base for a water tank, was much frequented. More debris lay in front of the courtyard's south wall. Subsidence resulted in the riverside wall of the room added to the building's rear to tip outwards, and this certainly resulted in the room's collapse. Over the room's floor and that of the adjoining room stone roofing tile fragments lay beneath the building debris that extended over their walls. A doorway that had accessed the addition was then sealed using roughly laid flint-blocks. Likewise, the access to the entrance hall at the east end of the courtyard had been blocked following that room's collapse. Demonstrating this the south wall had slightly tilted inwards and part of its south-east section had sunk into the fill of an underlying ditch. Levelled debris extended throughout the room, spreading out the wide entrance and along the room's frontage. Over the debris tail a flint gravel yard surface had been laid, extending eastward.

Behind the courtyard's southern building kitchen waste such as pottery fragments, bone, and oyster shell had been thrown into the boundary ditch. It incorporated much destruction debris including tesserae and wall-plaster. West of the building the upper part of the partially silted-up abortive well pit, left open since work ceased on the failed bath suite, contained comparable debris. Likewise, after destruction of the flooring the infill of the hypocaust of the finished bath suite contained much debris as did the stoke pit, where the debris also included half a sandstone dwarf column. A cobbled floor in the warm

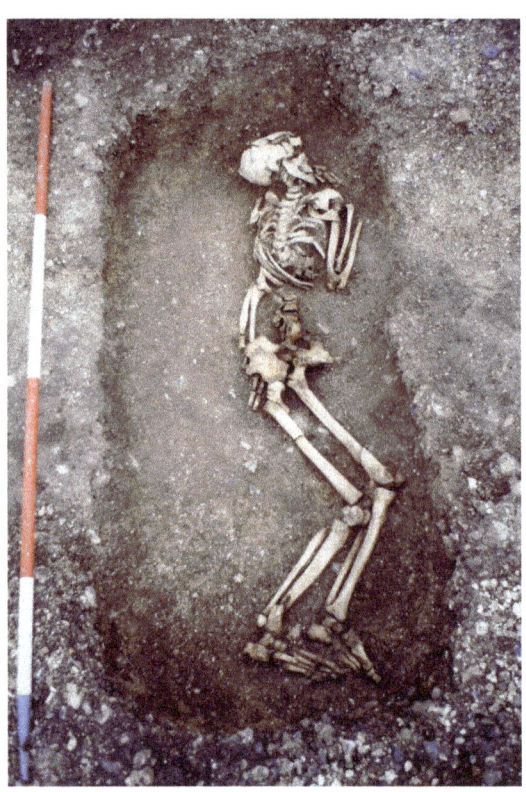

*Fig. 41. Late Roman/post-Roman burial from behind the southern building*

room containing and sealing twelfth/thirteenth-century pottery showed that part of the building was still standing at a very much later date.

On the gatehouse track a spread of stone roofing tiles and fragments either represent demolition debris or a rough re-surfacing. However, eventual demolition or collapse is shown by a spread of building debris in the gatehouse's south tower and on the east side of the building.

Much of the debris from around the courtyard had been disposed of in convenient hollows such as partly silted-up ditches and robbed hypocausts, which perhaps point to a continued attempt to maintain order. Better building material may have been removed by people for use on sites elsewhere where the trappings of Roman culture were being maintained.

Despite the evident collapse, demolition and decay the desire for, or use of, finer quality items remained. From the early fifth-century midden at the north end of the house pottery fragments included a variety of New Forest wares, most notably painted parchment ware bowls. Production on many kiln sites had seemingly ceased at the time the midden was forming, due to the poor economic situation and lack of coinage. So it is probable that the New Forest products were the last of a failing mass production industry, or remnants of a supply purchased earlier before production ceased. The latter may be the most likely, as the midden contained several handmade vessels, and in addition from the top of it came a knife of possible post-Roman date. Also, from within the midden there were many glass bowl, beaker and flask fragments which may likewise represent the remainder of the house's stockpile.

A final act for the late-Roman or immediate post-Roman period was the cutting of a grave through the infilled boundary ditch at the southern building's rear. This held the remains of an elderly (50+), 1.68-metres (5' 6") tall male who had evidently had a hard-working life which caused mild to severe osteoarthritis of the spine, shoulders, and knees. His left knee was particularly affected, and this would almost certainly have been painful – even in those robust days – with instability and giving way, requiring a stick or crutch for safe walking. A healed fracture of the right leg fibula is also indicated. During life he lost six teeth, two at an early age, with the remaining teeth becoming well-worn over time. Severe infection of one tooth in the upper jaw had resulted in a large abscess which would have drained pus into his mouth.

## II
## Saxon and Early Medieval Settlement (AD450-1150)

**Conflict and Turmoil**
The period between the end of Roman rule and the emergence of Saxon kingdoms was a time of conflict and great turmoil. Many regular troops had been withdrawn from Britain to protect Rome's heartland during the latter years of the fourth century AD and in the early years of the fifth century AD. Various usurpers were declared Emperor in Britain by the military, and this resulted in troops accompanying the usurpers to the continent as they sought advancement in territory and power in Gaul and beyond. Amongst the usurpers were Magnus Maximus (AD 383-8), Marcus (AD 406-7), Gratian (AD 407) and Constantine III (AD 407-11). Few if any of these troops returned. Consequently, the country's defences were much weakened at a time when the regular and militia armed forces were trying to repel raids by Germanic warriors on the south-east coast, Pictish warriors to the north and to the west Celtic warriors from Ireland.

Britain had stopped minting its own coinage in AD 326 and so relied thereafter on Gaulish mints for supply. The issue of bronze coins to Britain ceased in AD 402 and silver and gold coins in AD 406. Accordingly, coinage in circulation dwindled and this resulted in the breakdown of a functioning monetary system that had been relied on to pay for goods, services, and taxes. People now had to rely on self-subsistence, barter, or bullion to survive. Therefore, mass production industries such as pottery manufacture ceased to operate. Skilled workers such as masons, carpenters, mosaicists, and metal workers could not be paid, which resulted in the structural decay and eventual collapse of buildings, particularly those built in stone. Undoubtedly breakdown in government control and social order quickly followed.

Further deterioration within settlements and villas occurred due to the raiding war-bands, brigand activity and periods of plague. Adding to the unstable situation, foreign mercenaries hired by leaders of towns in eastern Britain rebelled against their employers. Thus further

*Fig. 42. Liddington Castle an Iron Age hillfort refortified in the post-Roman period*

destabilised, Britain's defences were unable to repel Germanic tribes (Saxons, Jutes and Angles) who, seeking fertile land on which to settle, joined with the rebels. The number of these incomers is debatable, but they were enough to introduce a new language, the basis of which we speak today (Hill 2003). Land was clearly taken, and the former owners were either slaughtered, enslaved, or driven out, while lesser folk such as the tenants of the former landowners may have submitted to the newcomers' rule, simply swapping one property-owner for another. Gildas, a British cleric, penned a sermon *De Excidio et Conquestu Britanniae*. Although written over a hundred years after the events the sermon records some grains of truth regarding the happenings of that traumatic period. He notes:

All the major towns were laid low by the repeated battering of enemy rams and laid low too all the inhabitants – church leaders, priests and people alike as the swords glinted all around and the flames crackled.

Self-subsistence for the remaining Romano-British people was easier to achieve in the countryside where arable land was available, so partial or total abandonment of large settlements took place. Notably some nearby hillforts such as Liddington Castle and Barbury Castle appear to have been refortified at this time, suggesting that some of the local population had retired to them as places of safety. Gildas records:

> ...the cities of our land are not populated even now as they once were, right up to the present they are deserted, in ruins and unkempt.

As evidenced by cemetery sites and recovered artefacts the Germanic tribes initially occupied the east of the country and then advanced inland along the Thames and Kennet Valleys.

**Saxon Occupation**
The distribution of finds relating to the Anglo-Saxon settlement, solely found in the north-west corner of the excavated area, clearly indicate that only the outer limit of Anglo-Saxon activity had been encountered. These items comprise six chaff-tempered pottery sherds, two late Roman coins pierced for use as jewellery and various carved bone tools that confirm another location for the growing number of sites occupied in the early Saxon period in the region. How early and for how long though is on present evidence difficult to determine as Saxon chaff-tempered pottery is difficult to date and spans a period from mid fifth century to early

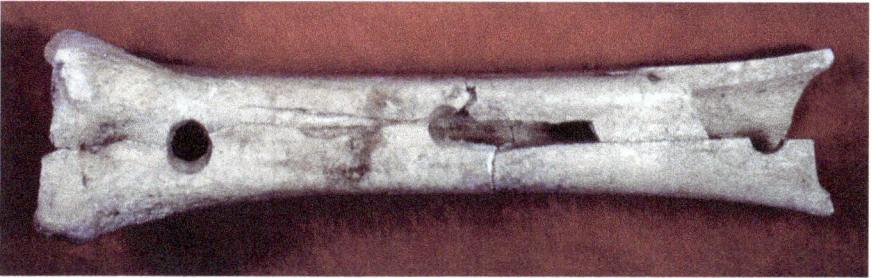

*Fig. 43. Saxon bone bobbin from Littlecote*

eighth century. However, it is reasonable to say that manufacture of woollen cloth took place, demonstrated by the carved bone implements found – bone comb fragments, a thread picker, a pin and ten possible bobbins (MacGregor 1985). The latter are shaped and drilled lower limb bones of cattle (*metapodials*). Much fuller's earth was also present in a ditch connected with some of the bone artefacts. It remains unknown whether the artefacts represent continued occupation by the former villa inhabitants, contemporaneous occupation by both British and Anglo-Saxon people, Anglo-Saxon occupation after the removal of the former occupants, or reoccupation following a period of abandonment.

**Early Medieval Occupation**

Although no buildings were traced for the early medieval embanking of the riverside with flint-blocks, three small pits and a shallow timber-lined well associated with tenth-century pottery fragments provide evidence for a continuation of settlement. A scatter of ninth- to early twelfth-century pottery sherds spread over much of the excavated area also supports this. Whether these remains point to a single farmstead or a larger settlement is unclear, but iron slag, an antler thread picker and lumps of fuller's earth found in one of the pits point to iron working and a continuation of woollen cloth manufacture.

*Fig. 44. Part of a wooden bucket from the tenth century well*

Littlecote lay within the Hundred (manorial holding of 100 hides) of Ramsbury, which was a West Saxon Bishopric estate created in AD 909. Unfortunately, the Domesday Book of 1086 records the Hundred under a single entry, individual settlements not being noted. It states that there was land for 54 ploughs, meadow 80 acres, pasture 14 furlongs long and 5 furlongs wide, woodland 16 furlongs long and 4 furlongs broad (Morris 1979). However, the excavation findings have clearly shown that Littlecote was in existence during this period.

*Fig. 45. Tenth century well at Littlecote*

Of note are the Domesday records for the small manor of Chilton in Kinwardstone Hundred, a village on the opposite riverbank to Littlecote. There was land there for 12 ploughs, meadow 2 furlongs long and 1 furlong wide, pasture as much, and woodland 1 league long and 2 furlongs wide. By contrast neighbouring Leverton, described in AD 984 as eight *mansae* (houses) beside the river, comprised land for four ploughs and woodland for two swine (Morris 1979).

## 12
# Littlecote: a Medieval Village (AD1150-1450)

**Setting and History**

Revealed by mounds and hollows in uncultivated grassland and partly levelled grassland, the earthworks of the medieval village of Littlecote stretches westward from Littlecote House for 650 metres. At least twelve building plots are discernible with their land divisions stretching from a partly sunken trackway to the southern bank of the River Kennet. Excavation revealed that buildings were concentrated close to the track with their work areas, animal penning and gardens behind.

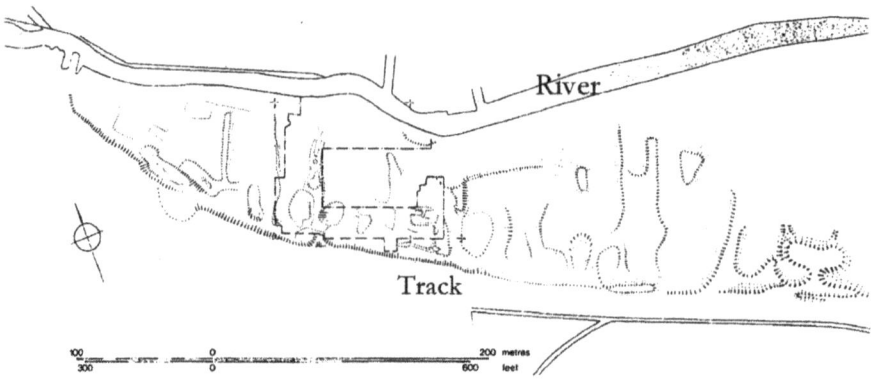

*Fig. 46. The earthworks of the medieval village*

The village would have been surrounded by the manor's farmland arable, pasture, water meadow and woodland. Regrettably, being part of the contiguous Ramsbury Hundred held by the Bishop of Salisbury meant that records relating to the village and its precursor are for the early period non-existent and subsequent records are rare. Thus, little is known about Littlecote's economic history or the villagers themselves. So, it is to the archaeological evidence that we must turn to provide a glimpse of the people, their work, and their homes.

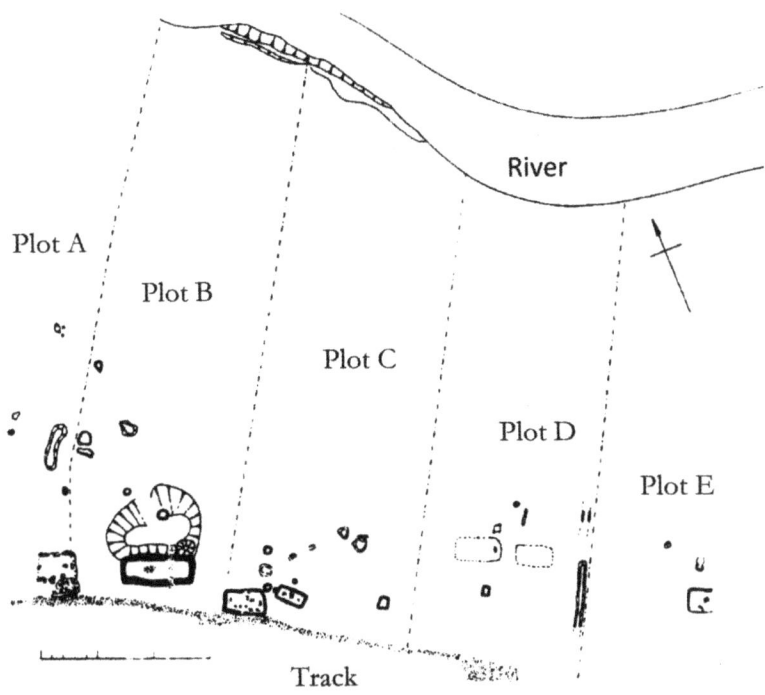

Fig. 47. The village c. AD 1200

Pottery and coinage found during the excavation suggest that the village had been fully established by the mid twelfth century which was a time when settlement expansion, due to population growth, was common. The nearby settlement of Ramsbury also appears to have been undergoing a similar expansion during this period (Croucher 1986).

The first written evidence for settlement at Littlecote is in the Pipe Rolls of 1182 when the manor was in the hands of Richard of Durnford (Crowley 1983). Following Richard's death in 1189/90 it passed to his son Roger. It remained with the family despite several claims on it until at least 1258. Littlecote then passed into the hands of Roger de Calstone and on his death in 1292 it became the property of his one-year-old son Roger. In 1328 Roger settled Littlecote on his marriage to Joan; it was conveyed with the advowson of the manor chapel. By 1334 the Littlecote tithing (ten households) had been established. In the same year Edward III was entertained at the manor. Roger's son Lawrence, after his father's death in about 1342, inherited the estate. In 1355 Lawrence granted all his lands to his son Sir Lawrence. Littlecote, when held by

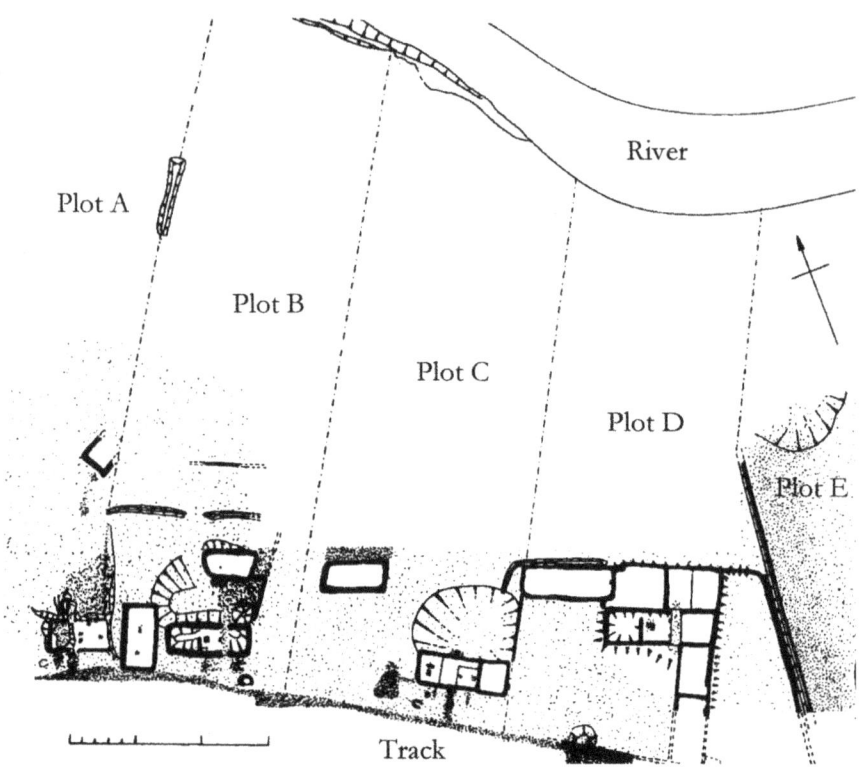

*Fig. 48. The village c. AD 1400*

Thomas, Lawrence's son born in 1385, was valued at 10 pounds per annum (roughly £10,000 today). Thomas had died before the marriage of Elizabeth, his daughter and heir, to William Darrell in 1419. William died between 1439 and 1453. Following Elizabeth's death in 1464 the estate passed to her son Sir George Darrell. Through George's first marriage he was the great-grandfather of Jane Seymour, future Queen of England and third wife of Henry VIII.

Around about this time the 'Status Conscious' began to build exclusive hunting parks surrounding their manor houses and it seems, as demonstrated by the lack of late medieval/early post-medieval pottery and coinage, that Sir George Darrell did likewise. During this time he evicted the villagers and demolished the village. The Park's success is demonstrated by the fact that Henry VIII had 'goodly pastimes and continual hunting' there in 1520.

## 13
## Littlecote: a Medieval Village – The Archaeology

Five medieval land divisions, designated A to E, defined by earthworks overlying the Romano-British villa remains and representing about one fifth of the village extent, were partly investigated during the excavation. Revealed were traces of thirty-one buildings of varying construction, size, usage, and date.

### Plot A

Fronting onto the main cobbled trackway a small post-built rectangular cottage (Bld. 6) was in the latter half of the twelfth century the home of a blacksmith and his family. On the building's southern side a central entrance opened into a single 4.4-metres by 6.1-metres earthen floored room that had near its eastern end a clay hearth. A porch was eventually added to the entrance along with, on its east side, a 2.18-metres by 3.5-metres room that probably served as a bedroom. From its compacted chalk floor came a small, decorated, silver penannular brooch. Bounded in part by linear mounds of flint-blocks, the plot to the rear of the building enclosed remains of two iron ore smelting furnaces. Surrounding these was an exceptionally large amount of iron smelting waste which included lumps of furnace bottom and run and tapping slag. Further down the plot nearer the river another furnace or smithing hearth was discovered in a timber structure, probably a smithy. Here farming equipment could be made and repaired, horses shod, and weapons, nails, household items, and building fittings forged.

By the mid thirteenth century the plot had passed into the hands of a tenant farmer who erected over the dismantled timber building a 4.4-metres by 10-metres two-roomed longhouse (Bld. 2). Flint-block walling enclosed the three external sides of the western room. The walls' narrow width indicated that, like many of the narrow walls of other buildings excavated, it was a dwarf wall serving as a base for a timber framework with wattle and daub infill. Flooring the room

*Fig. 49. Longhouse (Bld. 2), plot A*

compacted chalk overlaid a flint-block-filled sump from which a drain extended through the north wall before entering a large cess pit. These features clearly show that this room had been a byre for the housing of animals, presumably a pair of draught oxen or horses. From the cess pit came a thirteenth-century cooking pot, and sieving soil from the pit fill recovered charred barley, oats, wheat grain, and celtic bean. Written sources indicate that celtic beans were a vital component of medieval diet in Europe. They were particularly valued as a protein-rich food amongst poorer populations, thus serving as a substitute for meat (Moffett 2006). Sieved plant seeds from the pit were dominated by oat grass, brome grass, vetch pea and wild pea. These are plants typical of grassland, field margins, and arable environments. A gravel-floored cross passage separated the byre from the living quarters, an earth-floored room that contained a pitched sandstone oven base and two hearths, one positioned centrally the other against the room's north wall. This room was initially walled in clay and later replaced by a timber frame structure with its wall posts set on stone pads and sill beams resting on flint-block dwarf walling.

From the buildings front entrance, a path of packed small flint-blocks led from the cross passage to the trackway. On its west side remains of a bread oven were found. From the cross-passage rear doorway a flint-block paved ramp descended into an extensive drainage hollow and connected with a causeway of flint-blocks that extended across the hollow. Such hollows were also found on three of the other excavated village plots showing that heavy rainfall caused problems from flooding. From the building's north-east corner, a flint-block boundary wall stretched towards the river. A small pit containing the articulated skeletons of two cats and the cess pit were sealed when the drainage hollow was packed with flint-blocks. This layer extended up to the longhouse's north wall and overlay the largely dismantled boundary wall.

**Plot B**

To the east in the adjacent plot and fronting onto the trackway a 12.4-metres by 5-metres longhouse (Bld. 4) was erected in the mid twelfth century. Its well laid wide flint-block outer walling implies that it was built in stone up to the eaves. Its rear wall slightly overlapped the edge of an exceptionally large gravel-floored drainage hollow. Post pads edged the buildings front and rear doorways, between which a cross-passage was floored with small flint-blocks. Other post pads defined

*Fig. 50. Longhouse (Bld. 4), plot B*

the location of cross-screens either side of the passageway. East of the passage a 4.5-metres by 3-metres byre contained a flint packed sump that drained, via a channel beneath the north wall, into a large shallow pit. The byre was re-floored initially with crushed chalk then by compacted loam and finally gravel. West of the corridor, a large living room had a central 0.97-metre by 1.03-metres clay hearth. Having a doorway at its northern end a timber screen identified by a line of flint-blocks later divided the room into living and sleeping quarters. Both rooms were then floored with beaten earth before a sandstone-slabbed hearth was placed centrally in the living area and a flint-block base was laid next to its southern wall.

From the building's front door, a path of flint fragments led to the trackway and from the rear entrance a stone and broken Roman terracotta tile-surfaced ramp descended into the drainage hollow. A porch was added to the house front but was soon demolished and then in front of the byre a flint-block walled bread oven was built. At the building's rear an eastern boundary wall for the plot extended northwards from the building's north-east corner. The adjacent drainage hollow had cut into it various pits. Containing a glazed mid-thirteenth century jug one of the pits predated the erection of an 8-metres by 4.5-metres building (Bld. 5). Narrow, flint-block dwarf walling implies that this building, a small barn/workshop, had an upper timber frame. The area between the two buildings was, subsequently, partially cobbled with flint-blocks. At some point this building was demolished and a 5.2-metres by 9.8-metres building (Bld. 3) erected end on to the trackway, between the longhouse and the plot's western boundary. Its narrow flint-block dwarf walls tapered inwards, suggesting that they too had supported a timber-framed construction. Inside two clay hearths overlay a gravelled floor.

**Plot C**
Close to the trackway a short length of flint-block walling was all that remained of the earliest structure (Bld. 14) erected in the neighbouring eastern plot. Around the end of the twelfth century, on the opposite side of the plot and bordering the track, a slightly curved shallow drainage ditch was dug that later incorporated a rectangular sump. North of, and aligned with, the ditch a 5.25-metres long 2.6-metres wide and 0.3-metre-deep flat-bottomed hollow was identifiable as a sunken-

floored building (Bld. 10). Internally, bits of narrow flint-block walling survived at its edges, undoubtedly laid as a base to carry the sill beams of timber-framed wattle and daub walling. Three hearths were shown by traces of burning inside the building and the biggest lay at the centre. It is feasible that this single roomed structure functioned as a workshop or kitchen separated from the house due to the potential fire risk.

The ditch and sump had completely silted up prior to the hollow of a larger sunken-floored building (Bld. 9) being dug through it. It was located a little west of Bld. 10 with its frontage directly on, and aligned to, the trackway edge. Traces of narrow clay-bonded flint-block walling, set on ledges around its 4.2-metres by 8.5-metres and 0.25-metres-deep hollow undoubtedly served as a foundation for sill beams like Bld. 10. Post pits defined the position of opposing entrances, presumably linked by a cross-passage. A hearth was located within the western room, central to and abutting the surmised cross-passage wall. In the area to the east of the likely passage a hearth lay on the building's south side and various patches of compacted chalk set within shallow cuttings may have been bases for internal posts. Later a pale brown clay floor was laid throughout the building. Over this, on the west side of the former likely cross-passage, a timber cross-screen is indicated by a thin linear flint-

*Fig. 51. Sunken-floored building (Bld. 9) plot C*

block foundation and stone post pads, so dividing the building into two clearly defined rooms. The larger eastern room was the living area. It contained a compacted chalk-filled shallow hollow adjacent and central to the cross-screen, that probably served as a base for a post or other feature, and a clay hearth(s) that was re-located many times. Seemingly a bedroom, the smaller western room had a slight area of burning positioned close to the north-west corner, and cut into the north-east corner a small shallow pit contained a neonatal infant burial.

To the building's east lay another small building (Bld. 13). Its flat-bottomed 2-metres by 2.85-metres and 0.17-metre-deep hollow cut the flint walling of the earliest structure on the plot (Bld. 14). Size, isolation, and no internal features make its function uncertain, but perhaps it was a privy.

*Fig. 52. Farmhouse (Bld. 8), plot C*

To the rear of the trackside buildings a large quarry pit had provided the clay used to re-floor the largest sunken-floored building. The pit was subsequently used to dispose of refuse that included ash and carbonised grain. Other pits of varying size found close to Bld.10 included two that exhibited signs of burning and contained ash and burnt flints. These pits, using heated stones and hot ashes, were employed for cooking, baking and perhaps also for the making of malt. Sieving ash from their infills produced a large quantity of charred barley and a little wheat and oat grain.

Demolition of the sunken-floored buildings and infilling their hollows followed. Over the eastern sunken-floored building (Bld. 13) the erection of a 4.5-metres by 5-metres flint-block walled building (Bld. 8) took place that partially overlay the remains of a Roman building. Its narrow walling suggests that these were dwarf and supported a timber, and wattle and daub framework. Internally it was floored with a packed layer of small flint-blocks, chalk, and gravel. At the western end a flint-block dwarf-walled extension lengthened the building to 13.6-metres. Features within it identify the building as a cottage and these included, at the extension's west end, a chalk-floored hearth, a sump, traces of a thin compacted chalk floor and an oven base made from Roman tiles. Adjoining the extended building's rear an extensive drainage hollow was dug. Subsequently the extension appears to have been divided by timber partitions into three rooms and a corridor. These were defined by changes in flooring material. One area floored with gravel contained two hearths whilst in the building's western part the hearth was re-floored in tiles. Next to this, seven silver pennies of Richard II (reigned 1377 to 1399) had been hidden. A much-disturbed flint-block walled addition to the front of the building may have comprised two rooms floored in compacted chalk. Following the front addition's subsequent demolition, a gravelled path was laid extending from the cottage to the trackway. A little to the west of this lay a circular flint-filled sump and traces of a bread oven that underlay a mound of glazed terracotta roofing tiles and flint-blocks derived from its demolition. Extending towards the river from the building's north-east corner a free-standing flint-block wall had served as the plot's eastern boundary.

Set further back in the plot, overlying the now infilled clay quarry pit, construction of a 10-metres-long and 4.3-metres-wide barn (Bld. 7) had taken place. The thickness of the flint-block walls indicates that these had stood up to the eaves in stone. To its rear a layer of medieval terracotta roofing tile fragments, conceivably derived from the barn's eventual demolition, overlay flint-block paving that adjoined its rear wall.

## Plot D

Activity within the plot began in the second half of the twelfth century. Initially this consisted of a sequence of nine sunken-floored structures and culminated in the fifteenth century as a complex of linked flint-block dwarf-walled and timber-framed buildings.

Set well back from the trackway the early remains generally were fragmented due to successive construction being focused in the same area. The hollows of the sunken-floored buildings varied in depth from 6- to 32-centimetres. Little evidence remained of the upper structure of these buildings, but they were probably timber-framed with wattle and daub infill set on timber sill beams or low flint-block plinths and roofed in thatch or shakes.

The earliest structure (Bld. 25) had a chalk floor overlain central to its east end with a hearth, so identifying it as a domestic dwelling. Seemingly contemporary and a little to the east, a building (Bld. 26) had a yellow clay floor. Behind them a cooking pit, a baked-clay hearth and a sleeper beam trench are probably associated. Aligned north to south a wide shallow ditch extended past the east side of the eastern building and continued after a short break towards the trackway. Parallel to the ditch

*Fig. 53. Well, plot D*

a second ditch commenced in front of the building near to its western end. Post-dating the features at the building's rear, and most likely the second building also, a very large hollow of a building (Bld. 27) was cut and floored in compacted chalk, flint-blocks and gravel. Sealed by this were fragments of a mid-thirteenth century lead glazed jug. Cutting the eastern part of the structure Bld. 27 the hollow of a building (Bld. 28) was in due course replaced by another building (Bld. 24) that had a compacted earth floor. Overlying this a long rough linear grouping of flint-blocks appeared to be tumble from a wall. The western part of Bld. 27 was also dug through to create a large rectangular hollow for a building (Bld. 23) which was floored with a brown loam. This building was eventually cut by the hollows of three further buildings (Bld. 21, 22 and 23). Later, overlying the infill of Bld. 23 a layer of light yellowish-brown clay was laid as bedding for a wall of which four flint-block courses remained. On the wall's west side an associated hollow (Bld. 20) cut through the remains of Blds. 21 and 22. On this structure's north and west side connecting drainage channels were cut and within these brown silty loam accrued. Cutting the infill of the northern gulley a 2.15-metres-deep rectangular well pit was dug. Post pits at the corners show that it had an upper timber surround. From its lower silting came articulated bird and lamb skeletons, a sheep's skull, a small pottery cooking pot and a lead glazed lamp. Sieving of the silt revealed fruit pips, wheat and barley grain, eggshell, and plant seeds. Overlying the silted-up well, probably concurrent with Bld. 20, were traces of flint-block dwarf walling the base for a large timber-framed wattle and daub structure (Bld. 11). This 5.3-metres-wide by 14-metres-long single roomed building's end walls had centrally single large sarsen stones. These were presumably pads to support the posts holding the roof's ridge beam. No internal features were present in the building which was floored with a mixture of gravel, flint fragments and brown loam. Extending alongside the building's rear, a ditch stretched into the adjacent plot C before turning south and joining the cottage's drainage hollow. This suggests that drainage of the structure was imperative, and along with the building's size it points to it being a barn/sheepcote. Demolition of the adjacent building (Bld. 20) then occurred. Its eastern wall however was retained as part of a 5.24-metres-long and 3.6-metres-wide flint-block dwarf walled and timber-framed structure (Bld. 15). Most likely a store or workshop this building was linked to the barn/sheepcote's (Bld. 11) north-west corner through an extension of its northern wall. A thick loam floor was laid inside the building and an area of compacted chalk fronted it. Aligned north to south a ditch was cut in front of the barn/sheepcote a little south of its south-east corner heading to the trackway. This ditch was sealed when an extensive gravel yard was laid in front of the building. Later, cutting through the yard close to the barn/sheepcote a 1.5-metres by 1.28-metres and 2.58-metres-deep rectangular well was dug. It contained, towards the bottom a layer of cut timbers and branches. From this came a wooden roofing shake with its fastening nail, a pottery jug intact apart from a broken handle, an articulated cat

*Fig. 54. Sheepcote (Bld. 11), plot D*

*Fig. 55. Store/workshop (Bld. 15), plot D*

skeleton, and a long wooden implements handle. Sieving of overlying and underlying silt produced a variety of plant seeds, eggshells, and fruit pips. Above this clay and flint-blocks were used to purposely infill the well.

Fronting the plot at the northern edge of the flint-block-packed trackway a shallow gulley had been cut. Overlying its ensuing brown silty loam fill a slight earthen linear bank was raised encroaching onto the track's edge. Partly overlying the bank and constructed of clay bonded flint-blocks a free-standing bread oven was erected. Incorporated in its eastern side a smaller oven exhibited a heavily burnt interior. Added later to the structure's northern side a flint-block-constructed malting oven also showed much burning from use. Against the bread oven's western side, a thin ash layer accrued spreading over a wide area, which suggests that the oven was operated from that side. Later, extending over this narrow flint-block dwarf-walling incorporated the ovens at the centre of a building (Bld. 17), its southern wall stretching alongside the trackway. Ash from the bread oven's use continued to accumulate within the building's western part prior to the laying of a rough flint-block floor, the upper surface of which became worn and chipped through much tread. The building's eastern part comprised at least two rooms divided by a screen, evidenced by a rough line of flint-blocks with a gap for a doorway at its northern end. Within the western room abutting the bread oven a sandstone slab-based and clay surfaced hearth was constructed. Ash from its use, along with ash from the small oven and malting oven, had accumulated prior to the laying of a clay floor throughout the room. Burning on this indicated the location of two further hearths and patches of chalk that may be traces of a later floor. The room east of the screen had a floor of packed flint-blocks and fragments. Abutting the northern walls of the building

Fig. 56. House (Bld. 17), plot D showing bread oven, hearth, and malting oven

the gravel yard that also fronted the barn/sheepcote shows that the two structures were contemporary. The yard bore on its surface two deeply cut cartwheel tracks that extended from the barn/sheepcote towards the plot's south-east corner. Eventually, demolition of the building occurred, and its ovens' remains were sealed beneath a mound of brown loam. This followed the construction of a 5.75-metres by 19-metres longhouse (Bld. 16) a little to Bld. 17's rear.

The longhouse's (Bld. 16) mid-fourteenth century construction also overlay the second well following its infill, and the edge of the chalk fronting (Bld. 15). First, prior to the construction of Bld. 16's walling, a flint-paved ramp was built, and this led to a similarly floored surface which was to become the building's cross-passage. Then low banks of brown loam were formed at the rear, the western end, and an internal division to serve as a levelled base for the flint-block walling. The walls 0.56-metre- width suggest that they were built up to the eaves in stone. East of the cross-passage a room had a sequence of sumps but no drain or external cess pit, making it more likely that this was a store or service room rather than a byre. West of the cross-passage two rooms existed – a bedroom and living room separated by the internal clay bank which undoubtedly had supported a timber screen. A sequence of post pits clearly defined the location of a doorway that had accessed the screen at its northern end. Subsequently a line of small flint-blocks set on yellow clay formed the base for a replacement screen. The western bedroom contained a large flint-block packed sump, evidently an attempt to keep the room dry. Lack of overlying floor remains points strongly to the existence of a timber floor. Defining the boundary between the living room and the cross-corridor two largish stones set in pits functioned as posts pads supporting a cross-screen. Within the centre of the living room lay a square clay floored hearth. In due course it was surrounded by a gravel floor that extended throughout the cross-passage and into the eastern room. Inside the living room two small clay hearths were then set next to the north wall and a pit was dug near the south wall and infilled with flint-blocks. Presumably this was a sump or base for an internal feature such as a stand for a water container. A post pit cut through the central hearth was sealed by a pitched tile and stone hearth set on a clay base. Finally, encroaching slightly over the clay base, sealing the other features within the room, and abutting the cross-screen base, a gravel and loam floor was laid. From the building's north-east corner, a drainage ditch extended eastward into plot E. Dismantling of the store/workshop (Bld. 15) at the longhouse's rear enabled the building to be enlarged. This entailed the digging of a very large rectangular hollow immediately behind the building's eastern half. Around this and overlying the dismantled Bld. 15 low loam banking was raised, apparently to support walling that joined the house to the barn/sheepcote. A gravel cross-bank, presumably the base for a timber partition, divided the enclosed area created into two. The hollow, floored with brown clay, was later sub-divided, with the western part having a flint-block floor. From the enlarged building's north-east corner, a gulley was cut roughly parallel to the earlier drainage gulley.

In front of the longhouse an extensive packing of flint-blocks and fragments and brown silty loam contained many pieces of pottery. Over

*Fig. 57. Cess pit in Bld. 18, plot D*

this a well laid small flint-block and gravel yard lay beneath a compacted chalk layer that sloped up to, and abutted, the building's front wall and the west wall of another building (Bld. 18). Only partly dug, this flint-walled structure lay at right angles to the east end of the longhouse.

*Fig. 58. Building 18, plot D*

Separating the uncovered part of this building into two rooms a flint-block cross-wall ended a short distance from the eastern wall. Within the gap a small pit provided the setting for a door post. Central to the northern room's north end a 1.22-metres by 2.2-metres and 1.46-metres-deep rectangular cutting, identifiable as a cess pit, had its northern side walled in flint-blocks. On its base a thick deposit of charcoal-flecked silt contained articulated bird skeletons, eggshells and a late fourteenth/fifteenth century glazed lobed cup. Over this, deliberate infills of silt and flint-blocks contained an iron spur. Then followed the removal of the building's northern end wall, also the levelling of the internal cross-wall and the eastern wall. In place of the latter a shallow north to south flat-bottomed cutting was dug that accumulated yellowish brown silt. Eventually, over this and remnants of the former east wall, brownish yellow silty clay was laid as bedding for a wide clay bonded flint-block wall. This wall, seemingly, now linked with the longhouse, as is likely for an extended west wall. The southern part of the new wall was later removed, and its robbing trench infilled with a brown loam. In due course a narrower replacement flint-block wall was erected separated from the remaining part of the wide wall by an opening that provided access into the building. Erected between the building's outer walls a clay-bonded flint-block cross-wall was then built on the location of the former cross-wall. The northern room so created had an earthen floor laid within it. Later a cutting through the eastern wall and the digging of a post pit against its northern remnant provided a doorway into the southern room. The entrances through the east wall were subsequently blocked by roughly constructed flint-block walling. Following this, external to the east wall a gulley was cut that gradually filled with a silty loam. In the northern room adjacent to the blocked entrance a rectangular pit was cut, and this was in due course filled with brown silt and flint-blocks. Over this a thin narrow band of ash, charcoal and burnt clay lumps built up before the forming beside the cross-wall of a silty loam, gravel capped bank. External to the building against its east wall a similar bank was formed, and the earlier blocking of the entrances was apparently rebuilt. Within the southern room against its west wall a linear construction, perhaps for an internal feature, was erected prior to the laying of a thick silty loam floor that had slightly banked-up edges.

Fronting the plot adjacent to the trackway, and overlying the demolished south wall of the former building (Bld. 17), a low linear gravel and yellowish-brown loam bank was raised. On this there followed erection of a narrow free-standing flint-block boundary wall, against which banking-up of gravel occurred on both sides. Then the loam mound overlying the former ovens was capped with terracotta roofing tile fragments.

East of the longhouse and its eastern wing, after the longhouse's rear extension, creation of a very large triangular paddock occurred, apparently encroaching into plot E. It was bounded on the eastern side by a line of substantial, roughly rectangular fence post pits and a gulley. Subsequently replacement of the fence occurred with the building of an earthen bank, conceivably the base for a wall or hedge. The gulley was then recut, and a loam and gravel yard laid in the paddock. On the east side of the paddock's gully an extensive spread of gravel floored a large cutting that sloped down towards the nearby river. This perhaps created a track that led to a river crossing.

Linear mounds in the grassed area outside the excavated area define the full extent of the paddock. A trench cut into a small rectangular grassed mound at the south-western corner of the paddock indicated that it was a structure (Bld. 12) floored in clay. Its position and small size, 2.9-metres by 4.7-metres suggests that it may have been a dovecote.

**Plot E**
Fronted by a packed flint-block surface a slight flat-bottomed hollow 4.5-metres wide revealed the position of a rectangular house (Bld. 19), identifiable as such by an internal stone slab and clay hearth and a flint-block walled horseshoe-shaped structure which was perhaps the remains of a bread or malting oven. Filling the building's hollow following its disuse, or during its occupancy, a loam layer accumulated. Slightly north of the building an oven's keyhole-shaped firing chamber was located, lined with flints and sarsen stones.

*Fig. 59. Bread oven, plot E*

Around the mid thirteenth century, dug through the buildings eastern part and extending into unexcavated ground, an extensive hollow is comparable to drainage hollows at the rear of the houses in plots A, B, and C.

## 14
## The Village and Villagers

Littlecote during this period of history was one of many settlements scattered across the region, particularly along the stream and river valleys and sheltered coombes of the chalk downs. This very minor manorial settlement grew to consist of around twelve families plus the manor household. However, the artefacts recovered, buildings found, and the environmental evidence obtained during the excavation at Littlecote tell us much about the appearance, daily lives and beliefs of the folk inhabiting such rural settlements.

Throughout the period of the settlement's occupation external forces undeniably had varying effects on the inhabitants who depended on good harvests. Without doubt chief amongst these were weather and disease. Around the time of the village's conception records show that famine was prevalent, during 1150-4 and again in 1189-96, and during the years from 1315 to 1317 which was known as 'The Great Famine'. Reasons for this varied from periods of heavy rain to periods of drought. In 1158 it is recorded that at London the River Thames fell to a level that people could wade across, whilst severe flooding is recorded from 1199 to 1203 which caused meagre crop harvests. Drought meant that crop yield was poor and damage to fruit trees occurred, also that grazing was limited and likewise hay crops necessary to feed the animals over winter failed. Thus high animal and human mortality followed. In 1253 even mill streams dried up preventing the grinding of corn. Plague amongst humans was a recurring event causing high mortality; it was first recorded at the time of the village's occupation in 1175 and as pestilence in 1241 and 1251. Known as the 'Black Death', plague again broke out in 1348 and lasted until August 1350. Other outbreaks occurred in 1366 and 1479 (Stratton 1978).

Animals were susceptible to diseases which at times during the village's occupation were widespread. Records show that cattle plague was prevalent from 1313 to 1319. Sheep, a mainstay of the region, also suffered. In 1275 many sheep died from a disease thought to have originated in Spain. Outbreaks of sheep scab, a most contagious disease caused by parasitic mites, is referenced in 1277 and 1345. High mortality amongst domesticated animals also arose in 1283, and 1385 to 1389 (Stratton 1978).

Seeds, pips, and grain derived from sieving soil from the wells, cooking pits and a cess pit during the excavation tell of a long and well established open landscape of grassland, field margins and arable environments, with areas of wasteland and scrub in the village vicinity. They further reflect the usage of the land by the settlement's farmers with the cultivation of mainly wheat and barley but also of oat on the lighter calcareous soils which occupied the narrow flat strip of land between the River Kennet and the steep hillside to the south. Meadows located on the opposite side of the river were reached via a ford hinted at in the excavation east of plot D. Yielding firewood, autumn fruits, foraging for pigs and wild game, woodland that formed the north-eastern edge of Savernake Forest lay on top of the steep hillside to the south. The seeds, nut shells and fruit stones from the wells evidence wild plants, shrubs and fruit trees that could add variety to the villagers' diet. They include brassica, dock, common and small nettle, black bindweed, goosefoot, blackthorn, bramble, celtic bean, hazelnut, and apple/pear. Some of these plus other wild plants seeds identified – elder, campion, common bedstraw, corn gromwell, and poppy could have provided a source of medicine for the villagers as well as being used for dyes.

A total of 7,943 medieval animal bones were retrieved from deposits, mainly in well, pit and ditch fills. Included are the articulated (when uncovered) skeletons of wild birds, fowl, two lambs and three cats. Cats were undoubtedly kept as they helped to keep the rodent population down. Cattle and sheep bones dominate the assemblage, which suggest that occupants of the medieval village continued husbandry in a similar manner to that

Fig. 60. Cat and mouse, Luttrell Psalter c. 1325

evidenced for the site's former Romano-British, Anglo-Saxon, and Early Medieval inhabitants. Two deposits in plot D – one of the wells and the cesspit – produced domestic fowl eggshell fragments. Shells show that oysters were part of the villager's diet, as might have been a variety of fish, including eels, caught by traps set in the river. The nineteen iron arrowheads found on the site point to military training. In 1252 the Assize of Arms ensured that every man between the age of 15 to 60 years old should equip themselves with a bow and arrows. Edward III took this further and decreed in 1363 that the practice of archery must be held on Sundays and holidays. Perhaps relating to hunting, a tiny bronze rumbler bell from plot D could have been used in falconry. These were attached to a bird of prey's leg so that the falconer could hear the bird when out of sight.

Fig. 61. *Smithy as illustrated in a medieval manuscript*

Farming was certainly the primary function of the settlement. Cultivation however needed the support of other trades. Notable amongst these was the village blacksmith who would have made and mended farming equipment, shod horses and manufactured everyday items for agricultural work, building construction, and home. One blacksmith and his family lived and worked on plot A during the latter half of the twelfth and into the thirteenth century, manufacturing items from raw iron ore and scrap metal. His presence was shown by traces of the smithy, smithing hearth, smelting furnaces and a large quantity of iron slag. Other metalworking on a small scale is suggested by the finding of a small quantity of copper smelting waste, a clay crucible, and pieces of lead waste. A few coal lumps discovered also could relate to this industrial activity, and were obtained from exposed coalfields in the Avon and Somerset area.

Details of everyday domestic activities are clearly provided through the features discovered in and external to the houses and artefacts recovered. Cooking, baking, and brewing are evidenced through the hearths, ovens, baking/cooking pits and charred wheat, barley, and oat grains. Bread ovens in the thirteenth and fourteenth centuries were set between the house and track in plots A, B, C and D. Two of the ovens (plots B and D) were built of flint-blocks, consisting of horseshoe-shaped lower chambers that most likely providing fuel storage. Over this a domed chamber would have been heated up, then the hot ashes raked out or moved to one side to allow prepared dough to be put in and baked into bread. The other two (plots A and C) appear from the presence of burning at ground level to have an

Fig. 62. Bread oven as illustrated in a medieval manuscript

upper chamber that was heated from beneath. A small similarly built oven was incorporated in the side of plot D's bread oven. Behind the twelfth century house in plot E another form of oven was encountered having a keyhole shape, with its lower firing chamber having been dug into the ground and partly lined with flints and clay. This had clearly seen extreme temperatures and was fuelled by wood to heat its upper chamber. Of similar date three cooking pits were encountered – two in plot C and one in plot D. In these pits bread was baked, meat joints cooked, or fish steamed. Very hot fire-heated stones would have been placed on the pit's bottom to provide the warmth, and for steaming green vegetation was placed above to provide a moisture source. Then the food was put on top and finally the pit was sealed by placing branches across it then sacking and earth. Both pits in plot C contained carbonised grain – barley, free threshing wheat, and rye – perhaps also pointing to a malting function. A rectangular malting oven was added to the free-standing bread oven in plot D; later they were incorporated inside a building (Bld. 17). Bread ovens were mainly located

Fig. 63. Iron candlestick, as discovered

outside because of the potential risk of buildings catching fire. However, small ovens are identifiable in two houses adjacent to hearths. Hearths were an important feature of any house as they not only provided means of cooking but provided warmth and light. Lighting was also evidenced by the finding of an iron candlestick and two pottery lamps, the latter being of a type that would have been fuelled with animal fat. Gathered from the river edge bullrush stems stripped and dipped in melted animal fat and held in taper holders were another form of lighting commonly used in medieval homes.

Artefacts relating to food preparation and consumption recovered, other than pottery vessel fragments, include many iron knives, an iron cleaver, numerous whetstones, and pieces of stone and bronze mortars. The latter undoubtedly expensive items were used with a pestle to crush herbs for culinary and medicinal purposes. The absence of hand-operated quern stones used to make flour implies the existence of a miller and a watermill. In Domesday Book, 1086, it is recorded that in the Ramsbury Hundred, in which Littlecote lies, there were 10 mills. It is likely that those on the River Kennet were located at places where mills are later recorded. A mill is evidenced at Littlecote in the post-medieval period when in 1699 Mr Bigg paid one pound 'for the standing of his wares in the old mill pond'. In 1783 Thomas Cowley received 5 shillings for repairs at the mill (Somerset Archive and Record Service, DD\POT and DD\PO).

Cloth-making, mainly for the household's woollen clothes, is shown by the discovery of a wool comb, spindle whorls, shears, bronze and bone needles, a pair of scissors and a sacking needle. The finding of a glass pebble-shaped flax-rubber/linen-smoother, an uncommon item (used in the finishing and laundering of textiles and garments), hints at flax having been gathered to make linen. Other artefacts demonstrate further activities that the villagers were involved in, such as carpentry (by an axe, chisel, gouge, spoke-shave, and a hammer), and haulage and transport by 75 horseshoes, a linch-pin, and a spur. Iron keys, latch lifters, and lock parts demonstrate the need for security. Iron fixtures relating to buildings and furniture comprise door pivots, chains, a suspension chain with attached swivel, hinges, staples, a door catch, door studs, a wall hook, wall pins, and nails. Representing the villagers' personal wear, finds include a small, decorated, silver penannular brooch, penannular brooches of bronze and iron, several bronze finger rings, bracelets, bronze cloak/headdress pins with glass heads, and a garter hook. Commonest items though were bronze fittings for leather straps and belts which comprised buckles, plates, strap ends, decorative mounts, and a decorated swivel. Pointing to the need for tough leather footwear are many cleats, hobnails, and boot plates.

Various pottery vessel types were found that tell of food storage, cooking and serving. Included are cooking pots, jugs, bowls, skillets, dishes, a confectionery mould, and tripod pitchers. These had largely been produced on kiln sites located within the Kennet Valley, one of which was excavated near Newbury in Berkshire (Mepham 2000). The date range of this so called 'Kennet Valley' ware is from the eleventh century through to the early fifteenth century. From the mid fourteenth century this local ware was augmented by regional products in the form of white wares from the Surrey/Hampshire border area (Pearce and Vince 1988) and limestone-tempered wares from the Minety area in North Wiltshire (Musty 1973). Finewares include a slip-decorated Laverstock or Naish Hill jug and a small, glazed cresset lamp. Other glazed and decorated finewares are likely to derive from the Newbury area where at least one thirteenth-century kiln producing such wares was

excavated at Ashampstead near Reading (Mepham and Heaton 1995). An almost complete lead-glazed lobed cup found in plot D's cesspit came from the Surrey/Hampshire border kilns. Other whole, or nearly whole, pottery vessels include, from the wells on plot D, a small cooking pot and a jug. A large cooking pot was found in Bld. 4's cess pit and a curfew from the ditch at the rear of the likely barn/sheepcote (Bld. 11) on plot D. Curfews were large covers placed over a hearth's heaped hot ashes as a safety precaution,

*Fig. 64. Early fourteenth century 'Kennet Valley' jug from a well in plot D*

reducing the chance of sparks causing fires at night, but also to help keep the ashes glowing ready for the following day's fire. Besides wood and charcoal, peat may have been used as fuel. This was clearly dug in the early eighteenth century from the River Kennet's water meadows, as shown by an entry in the Littlecote Estate account books (Somerset Record Office).

The thirteen silver pennies and three bronze jettons dating from c. 1200 to c. 1400 discovered on the settlement rank high in total when compared to other rural sites in the country. A survey of thirty-three medieval village excavations revealed that coinage was only present on seventeen. From a total of sixty coins and nine jettons most sites produced only one, two, or three, but exceptional numbers were found at West Whelpington in Northumberland which produced eight, Lyveden in Northamptonshire had nine, and seventeen from Westbury in Buckinghamshire (Dyer 1997). Coinage would have been used to pay rent and for the purchase of a variety of items such as pots, clothing, shoes, belts, jewellery, animals, farming equipment and services such as those supplied by the village blacksmith, carpenter, and miller. However, many transactions were obtained through barter, particularly amongst the villagers themselves.

Five of the silver pennies found at Littlecote represent casual loss, the earliest is of Henry II (reign 1154-1189) and the latest of Edward I (reign 1272-1307). Dating to the reign of Richard II (1377 to 1399) the hoard of six silver pennies concealed by the hearth in Bld. 8 is unique in Britain due to its single monarch composition. It may therefore represent a single payment for goods or services. The finding of the

---

*An eleventh-century document, the Rectitudines or Rights and Conditions of Man, states that it was the lord of the manor who provided the farmer with his house, plot of land (7 acres) stocked with beasts (2 oxen, 1 cow and 6 sheep), tools and utensils. The farmer however, had to spend well over half of his working week on the lord's land and pay taxes. When he died, all he had was left to the lord of the manor (Harvey 1993). Villagers had basically to be self-sufficient, able to pay their dues in rent and service to their lord, then any surplus could be sold at market.*

two French/Tournai counters and a 'Sterling' jetton compares to those found on a lot of other village sites in small numbers. Their presence has long remained a mystery as they were primarily used for calculating payments on a chequer board. Plausibly, they may represent given or received unofficial small denomination payment such as at an alehouse, or that they were used as counters on board games (Dyer 1997). A further idea is that they represented religious amulets given to ward off evil, notably ones that bore the letters HIS [IHS?] or AVE MARIA (Gilchrist 2012, 166) as did a penannular brooch fragment found at Littlecote.

**Buildings**
Mostly the domestic buildings lay parallel to and very close to the trackway with ancillary structures set further back into the well-defined plot boundaries. Also, the plots would have contained penning for animals and fowl; a vegetable plot; perhaps an orchard of apples, pears, or plums; as well as work and storage areas.

All the plots exhibited development over the three hundred years that the village existed. Plot A, first housing the village blacksmith, was later possessed by a farmer as shown by the longhouse that replaced the smith's cottage. Three plots (B, C and D) can be seen to have developed gradually to present farm layouts – that is a domestic dwelling plus outbuildings that might include a barn, workshop, store, or sheepcote. One of these, plot D, revealed signs of more than average wealth – bigger structures, wells, quality vessels and finds telling at least in its later stages of a higher social standing than the other plot owners.

Varied styles and methods of building construction are presented within the village. These may indicate that the settlement grew over time as building methods changed, availability or costs of building materials, or building traditions of the owners. Self-sufficiency and self-reliance seemingly were the rule for the peasant in rural medieval England. The plot's owner, from quarrying within his plot or gleaning flint-blocks from the fields and timber from the woods, presumably with the lord's permission, obtained much of the building material he needed. One building in plot C was clearly partly constructed of material sourced from alterations to Littlecote's manor house, as its walls contained brick and encaustic tile fragments. Two carved stone window or door mullion fragments found in another building's wall probably derived from the same source. In plot A the blacksmith's cottage (Bld. 6) was the only structure solely of posthole and post pad construction. Its replacement longhouse (Bld. 2) had a byre with a flint-block plinth for timber, wattle and daub walling and a living area walled in clay which was later replaced by a timber-framed structure whose posts rested on sarsen stone pads. Of varying depth sunken-floored buildings appear early in the village's history, these being confined to plots C, D and E. Evidence for the walling of these buildings was slight. The sunken-floored buildings Bld. 9 and 10 in Plot C however showed that narrow clay-bonded flint-block plinths set at their hollows' edges had supported sill beams for timber, and wattle and daub walling. Substantially built, the longhouse within plot B (Bld. 4) was seemingly constructed from flint-blocks and Roman terracotta tile fragments gleaned from quarrying the villa house remains that underlay the plot. This and two other structures (Bld. 7 and 16) based on their thick walling are likely to have also been constructed up to the eaves in stone. By the mid/late thirteenth century building styles had become almost universally timber-framed with wattle and daub infill set on dwarf stone walls/plinths. One unusual form of construction was confined to the later buildings and freestanding walls of plot D. Here the flint-block walls were built on low earthen banks and existing walling had banking added on either side. Roofing evidence for the structures was lacking, implying that either thatch or wooden shakes were used. Wooden shakes were thin 7.6- to 20-centimetres-wide and 36- to 91-centimetres-long. One shake, still retaining its iron fixing nail, came from a well in plot D. The barn (Bld. 7) in plot C may have had a terracotta-tiled-roof, as numerous tile fragments were found on a flint cobbled surface at its rear.

Amongst the building types identifiable in the village there are three that can be classed as longhouses – Bld. 2 in plot A, Bld. 4 in plot B and, perhaps, Bld. 16 in plot D. These structures are recognisable in having a passage between the front and rear entrance which separated animal housing (byre) from the householders' living and sleeping area. Based on having internal hearths but lacking byres, six other buildings can be classed as cottages or farmhouses. Two cottages – Bld. 6 in plot A and Bld.8 in plot C – began as single-roomed structures with additions being made as fortunes changed or the family grew. Another cottage (Bld. 17) was an addition to existing free-standing bread and malting ovens. Three apparent cottages have sunken floors (Blds. 9, 19, and 25. Normally such structures are designated as weaving sheds, workshops, or stores (Chapelot and Fossier, 1985). Of the Littlecote sunken-floored cottages only Bld. 9 survived in its entirety. This like a longhouse incorporated a cross-passage with a room on either side. However, neither room had a sump or drain, a necessity for a byre, but contained hearths and

*Fig. 65. A timber-built sheepcote, Book of Hours of Duc de Berry 1409-16*

in the western room an infant burial. Clearly in this case the corridor divided a sleeping area from a living area. The adjacent single-roomed sunken-floored building (Bld. 10) had a large central hearth and may have functioned as a kitchen or workshop. Two buildings, Bld. 7 in plot C and Bld. 11 in plot D, due to their large size and lack of internal features are almost certainly barns for storage of produce and equipment, and

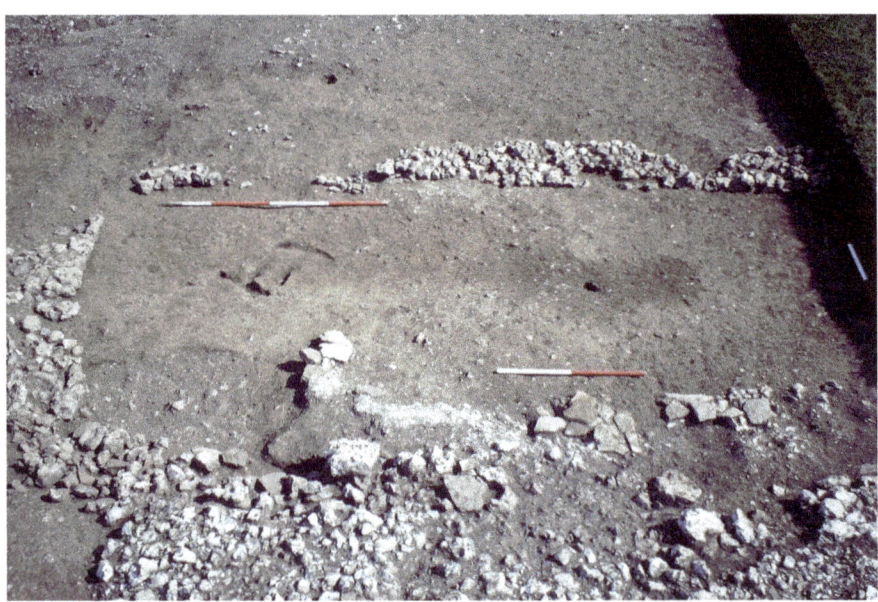

*Fig. 66. Store/workshop (Bld. 5), plot B*

perhaps for sheltering animals in bad weather. The latter floored with a mixture of gravel, flint fragments and brown loam may have been a sheepcote (*bercaria*). Drainage ditches to the rear and the west end would have kept it dry and, fronting it, a well implies the presence of animals that required regular watering. Of note is a well that pre-dated the building and which had two lambs' carcases and a sheep's head thrown into it. In an eighth-century AD account of sheep shelters it is stated that, by the rule of thumb, one square yard (0.84 sq. m) was sufficient housing for each sheep, thus Bld. 11 could have housed up to sixty sheep. Sheepcotes were used for winter shelter, fodder stores and lambing. Other single-roomed buildings to the rear of the houses are unlikely to have been barns due to their small size, but were stores or workshops, particularly Bld. 5 in plot B and Bld. 11 in plot D. The large building (Bld. 3) in plot B, floored with gravel and having two clay hearths, is difficult to categorise. Lack of obvious internal partitions and the presence of an adjacent longhouse, suggest that it was more likely a workshop such as would be needed for carpentry or a similar craft. Of at least two rooms Bld. 18 clearly exhibits several changes of use. Fronting but initially detached from the longhouse (Bld. 16) in plot D, it incorporated at its northern end a cess pit suggesting at least a partial domestic function. Later, entrances were inserted on the east side giving access to a fenced paddock. These were finally blocked, following which a little ash charcoal and burnt clay found in the northern room suggest a return to domestic or workshop activity.

Most villagers undoubtedly drew their water from the river at the rear of their plots and stored it in wooden tanks or barrels. Found in two of the houses, and perhaps indicating the presence of these, are stone and small chalk packed pits which could have functioned as both stand and drainage sump. Providing an alternative to river water, two wells found in Plot D were in use during two phases of its existence.

Drainage appears to have been an important consideration for the inhabitants. For most the threat of flooding was alleviated by the cutting of extensive drainage hollows to the rear of the houses. Bld. 4 had its drainage hollow dug in the twelfth century, while Bld. 6 and the later envisaged house in plot E had their hollows dug in the thirteenth century, and Bld. 8 had its hollow dug in the fourteenth century. Plot D however relied on ditches throughout its history, notably that which flanked the rear and west end of the barn/sheepcote (Bld. 11) and those that drained eastward from the house (Bld. 16).

**The Death of a Village**
Life had dramatically changed for the Littlecote villagers in the second half of the fifteenth century as shown by the lack of pottery, tokens, or coins of later date. Total abandonment and levelling of standing structures had occurred. What happened to its people can only be surmised. Did Sir George Darrell, the then owner of Littlecote House, in his quest for the pleasures and prestige of a hunting park, turf out his tenants to wander the country lanes or did he find them homes and land elsewhere? That the park was a success is shown by records that state that Henry VIII had in 1520 'goodly pastimes and continual hunting there'. Early parks which had aesthetic and social overtones also had an economic importance attained by grazing and the selling of game and timber. Documents relating to a park at nearby Ramsbury demonstrate this. There in the fourteenth century they refer to pasture, meadow, woodland, chase, and warren as well as rabbit, deer, swan, fish, pheasant, partridge, and hare (Somerset Archive and Record Service, DD\POT and DD\PO). Farming on Littlecote's holdings, however, still played an important part of the estate income as at some point in time a farm known as 'Park Farm' was established south-west of the house within the estate grounds. In 1549 it is recorded that over 700 sheep were kept and in 1589 wheat was sold for £52 and barley for £25.

# 15
# Post-Medieval Hunting Lodge (AD 1650-1780)

Two hundred years passed between the desertion of the medieval village of Littlecote and the erection of a cottage on its long-forgotten turf-covered ruins. During the intervening time Littlecote manor house had been transformed into an extravagant country mansion set within a 275-acre landscaped park, dedicated to the joys and pleasures of the wealthy.

*Fig. 67. English School, oil painting of house and hunting park c. 1730*

Capturing this scene an English School oil painting *c.* 1730, shows the mansion set within its park. Cameos depict many aspects of estate life including hunting of deer, fox and hare, fishing, and falconry. Various buildings are shown other than the mansion such as stables, a gatehouse, a dower house, a farm and on the riverside the afore-mentioned cottage.

Excavation of this brick- and flint-walled building, which based on finds and map evidence stood for around 130 years, revealed five phases of construction.

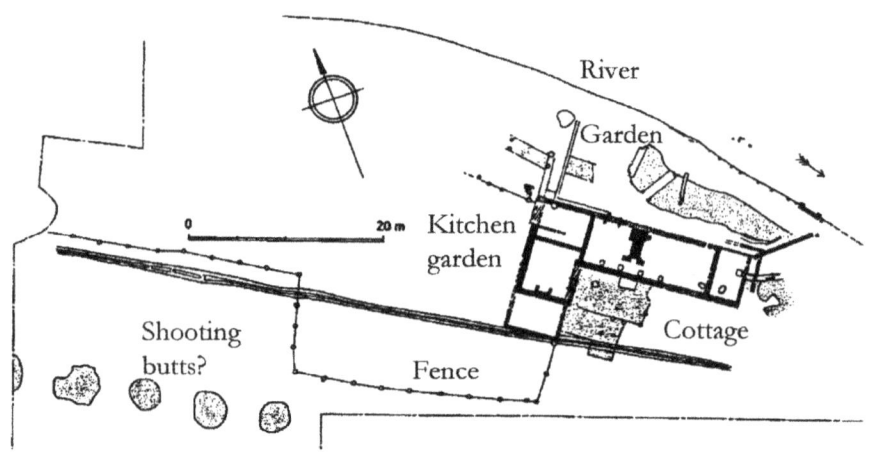

Fig. 68. The hunting lodge c. 1760

Erected shortly after the end of the 1642–1651 English Civil War it initially comprised a modest but comfortable brick- and flint-walled cottage having a terracotta-tiled roof (phase 1). Separated by a brick chimneystack two ground floor rooms and a small lobby existed with fireplaces opening into each. The largest served the bigger eastern room indicating that it was the kitchen/dining room with cooking taking place in the fireplace. The brick and tile floored western room was, seemingly, a sitting room. As seen in many cottages of this period and as indicated by its smaller fireplace, it is likely that the chimneystack incorporated a stairway which ascended from the room's north-east corner to an upper floor. Heating the lobby, the third fireplace was tiny.

In about 1670 a flint-block walled room was added at the eastern end (phase 2). Jutting out slightly from the building's rear this probably stood only a single storey high. It was replaced, c. 1690, in brick and flint-blocks (phase 3). From it emerged a brick lined drain implying that the brick floored room and conceivably its predecessor had functioned as a washroom. Abutting the room's walling and bordering the drain a flint cobbled surface extended around the rear of the building, where it was inset with a brick path. Underlying the well-worn path and cobbling a bedding of gravel, sand, terracotta tile and brick fragments contained an unworn trade token dated 1667.

Around 1710 at the opposite end of the cottage, construction took place of a north to south aligned wing comprising two rooms

# ARCHAEOLOGICAL EXCAVATIONS IN THE PARK

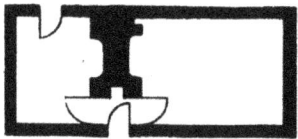

Phase 1, c. 1650

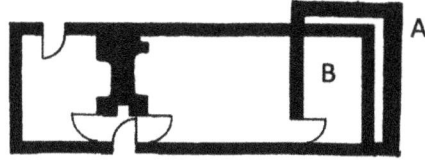

Phase 2 - A, c. 1670

Phase 3 - B, c. 1680

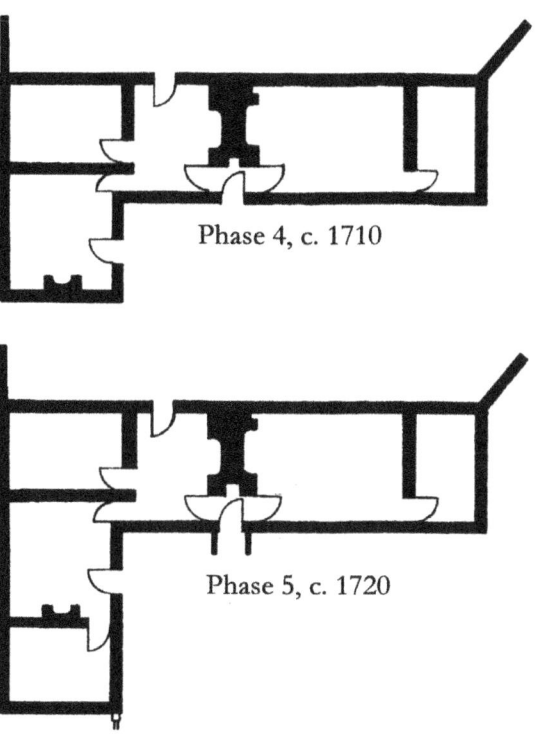

Phase 4, c. 1710

Phase 5, c. 1720

*Fig. 69. The hunting lodge phases of construction*

*Fig. 70. Excavated house on the c. 1730 oil painting*

(phase 4). The southern room had a fireplace and wooden floor and so must have served as a sitting room, whilst the previous sitting room may have become a dining room. An insight into the activities taking place in the room is provided by the discovery of numerous objects that fell through cracks between its floorboards into the floor well. Included are many clay pipe fragments, coins (Charles II to George II), marbles, dress making pins, a thimble, buttons, buckles, a musket ball, a gun flint and two jettons depicting Queen Anne (issued 1712 to 1714). The two counters were made by Johann Conrad Hoger who worked from 1712 to 1743 in Nuremberg, Germany. Jettons were thin copper coin-like tokens produced and used throughout Europe between the thirteenth and seventeenth centuries. Originally produced for use in calculating they were later used as a money substitute in gaming. This room could be entered internally, or directly from the front yard via doorways in the eastern wall. The northern room, perhaps a withdrawing room, appears to have had a staircase situated against the southern wall, evidenced by a single line of bricks. Between the house and the River Kennet a brick drain, flint cobbling and a flint-block path formed part of a formal garden. Clearly at this stage the status of the cottage had been upgraded.

Fig. 71. Early eighteenth-century Delft ware chamber pot from the river

A final flint- and brick-walled addition of a room at the southern end of the west wing took place c.1720 (phase 5). Accessed from the envisaged sitting room it may have been a study. It is at this stage of development that the building, now a substantial two storied house, can be seen on the English School painting.

Of note is a record in the estate accounts of building work taking place in the park. Dated 25 April 1719, 3,000 bricks and four quarters of lime are priced at £3-10s-00d. A later record refers on 9 May 1719, to 900 bricks and two buckets of lime at 17s 4d. These are allotted 'To ye Lodge'. On 11 June 1719 further accounts note 'James Field ye brick maker his bill as arranged £15-12s-00d, Thomas Phillips ye mason his bill as arranged £3-16s-01d and Samuel Dixon ye glazier his bill as arranged £2-07s-02d'. It is tempting to relate these building records to the construction of the cottage's southern room. However, there were many buildings on the estate, as depicted on various eighteenth-century maps, so the references could be to any one of them.

Around the same time the rear garden underwent enlargement with revetting and infilling that extended it out into the river. Now there were brick paths, flint cobbling and flowerbeds with, at both ends of the garden, brick walls to provide shelter and seclusion. West of the house and western garden wall a large area of deeply cultivated ground implies the presence of a kitchen garden. Beneath this lay the Roman Orpheus mosaic found in 1727. Indeed, a pile of Roman tesserae lay adjacent to the doorway through the formal garden's western wall.

*Fig. 72. Remains of the seventeenth/eighteenth century cottage/hunting lodge*

Traceable in the excavation as post pits set around the kitchen garden a fence line extending from the wing's south-east corner can clearly be seen on an estate survey of 1775 by Thomas Smith of Shrivenham. It also shows on a 1773 map of Wiltshire by Andrews and Dury. The enclosed western part beyond the vegetable patch may have served as an orchard or paddock.

Placing of the cottage on the river's edge may have been deliberate, chosen because of the firm ground provided unknowingly by the medieval river embanking and Roman ruins. The main reason, however, may have been due to a feature shown on a 1775 estate map, Andrews and Dury's 1773 map and a survey of Knighton Park c. 1790. Represented on the opposing riverbank is a large, channelled feature that on the c. 1790 survey is noted as a decoy. That feature is still discernible today as earthworks amongst scrubland, and appears to consist of an outer circular channel with six channels radiating out from a central circular channel as depicted on the 1773 map. As a decoy for waterfowl its form differs from the normal layout for such a feature. Typically, they consisted of a pool of water from which extended up to eight curving tapering ditches. Over each ditch known as "pipes" were set a series of hoops made from wood or iron that lessened in size as the ditch narrowed. These were covered in netting and on the outside curve of the pipe over-lapping screens were erected. As ducks are naturally curious when they see a predator, such as a fox, they will follow it keeping at a distance. Using a dog, the decoy man lured the ducks along the pipe until the ducks were trapped at the pipe's end. Notably in phase one of the cottage a timber footbridge was found to have extended across the river and later in the garden extension this was rebuilt, with on the river's south side a brick abutment. These suggest a link between the decoy and the cottage and that it also may have served as a keeper's residence with the keeper's primary function being to look after the river and the decoy. A line of five early eighteenth-century flint-block platforms, possibly flooring for shooting butts aligned parallel to the river was found in the excavation south-west of the cottage. Such butts could have been used to conceal hunters as they fired at wild fowl released from the assumed decoy. From the floor of one came a seventeenth century cast bronze miniature toy gun, capable of being fired.

Fig. 73. Seals from wine bottles from the river

Also hinting at a connection to the hunting aspect of the park are artefacts recovered from the building, its garden, and the adjacent riverbed. Included are: eight gun-flints, four lead musket balls, three brass wire snares and twenty-four hollow tubular lead weights, perhaps used to weigh down nets. Amongst the many pursuits depicted on the c.1730 painting is the hunting of a hare undertaken on horseback using nets, and using nets to catch fish in the river. Hunting is also evidenced by the 6,405 animal bones excavated, particularly those from the river silts. These largely comprise red and roe deer bones, of which all parts of the skeleton are represented, suggesting butchery of carcases taking place in the building, probably inside the washroom addition. Also, among the bones large dogs are represented. Many of these animals are shown on the *c.* 1730 painting including three hunting packs, two in the act of chasing foxes. Bones of horse and waterfowl are also present.

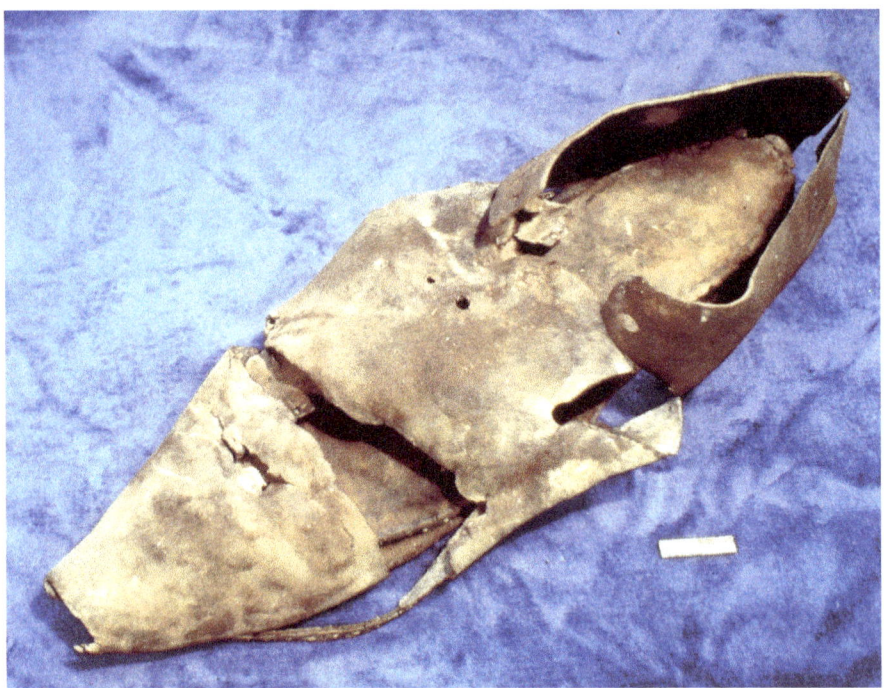

*Fig. 74. Late seventeenth century leather shoe from the river*

Throughout the building's life many items used in it remained on the site having been dumped into the river. These artefacts, which included leather and wood items, present a variety and abundance of material. Aided by the fact that the site was insular, excavation total, and no later contamination occurred they provide a rare illustration of life in a seventeenth- and eighteenth-century country household of a high social standing. Besides the hunting aspect, they provide a picture of domesticity, family, gender, leisure, status, health, dress, work,

*Fig. 75. Carved bone comb, whistle, and apple corer from the river*

transport, and travel, as well as providing information on the building's appearance and its fittings and fixtures.

Household items relating to the preparation of food and drink and its consumption include a wide variety of pottery vessels for cooking, table, and storage. Amongst them are bowls, tea bowls and saucers, a table salt, dishes, platters, posset pots, storage jars, jugs, skillets, porringers, tankards, an Italian costrel, basins, and chamber pots. A few wooden bowls and a wicker basket are also represented, as are a pewter porringer, a broad-rimmed pewter plate, and half of a cast iron cooking pot. Glassware includes small bowls, flasks, medicinal bottles, stemmed drinking glasses, tumblers, cruets, and numerous wine bottles. Some of the latter bear seals with the names of the estate owners and a date – Alex. Popham 1712 [born 1657, died 1718?] and Fran. Popham 1712 [born 1682, died 1735]. Another depicts a bear and crown which undoubtedly relates to the Bear Inn that the Pophams owned in nearby Hungerford.

Another is marked [Pyr]mont Wat[er] and originally this would have contained mineral water from Pyrmont in the German Province of Waldeck. This carbonated water was said to have undoubted efficiency

*Fig. 76. Early eighteenth century wood and iron mouse trap from the river*

in diseases of females, nephritic complaints, scrofula, rheumatism, and diseases of the eyes. Food related utensils comprise thirty-nine iron knives, some of which have bone, antler, and wood handles; a child's wooden knife with a carved, fish-shaped handle; whetstones; eighteen pewter and bronze spoons; three iron table forks with bone handles; two meat skewers; a cleaver; a ladle; a corkscrew; three bone apple corers and a wooden butter pat. The presence of an iron chamber stick, a wick trimmer, a strike-a-light and pieces of coal demonstrate lighting and heating within the building. Cleaning is shown through an iron hand shovel and remains of three wooden brushes, the hairs of which were once held in place with brass wire. Various lock parts and seven keys demonstrate the need or desire for security. Indicative of health problems are drug jars and salve pots, glass phials of varying sizes, and six wood and bone nit combs. An unusual item was a wooden mousetrap complete with iron fittings which effectively chopped off the rodent's head. Work items used in the house and gardens include iron saw blades, a gouge, a drill bit, files, wedges, pincers, an axe/hammer, trowels, chains, bucket handle, spade sheathing, scythes, a wood rake head and a wood pulley wheel.

Finds demonstrate that all genders and children lived in the building. Women, by four hundred dress making pins, bodkin, eleven pairs of scissors, nine thimbles, four wood and leather pattens and their iron bases, and glass beads. Men, by over 2,300 clay pipes, carpentry tools, three wig-curlers, a razor, eight folding knives, and leather boots with boot plates, as well as the items relating to hunting. Children are shown to have lived there by the presence of a skipping rope handle, writing slate, four lead writing sticks, small leather shoes, fifteen marbles, the decorated fish knife, and the miniature pistol. Of course, some of these items could be assigned to either gender. Artefacts relating to the apparel worn by these people were numerous, including

*Fig. 77. Watch key, jaws harps, tweezers, penknife, and a fob with seal from the river*

a wide range of leather shoes; leather belts; fifty-three belt and shoe buckles; and seventy-one buttons of silver, wood, bronze, bone, pewter, and lead. That the occupants of the building were well-off amongst the estate's inhabitants is shown by the fine pottery that includes porcelain, glassware, the wine bottle seals, a gold wedding ring, coins (six silver and thirty-eight bronze – Elizabeth I to George II) and a trade token issued by a silk weaver in Oxford. Additionally, a watch key and a glass fob seal engraved with a dove holding in its beak an olive branch and surrounding the words 'love peace' was found. This would have been worn suspended on a watch chain, which seems at odds with a hunting park. However, it is worth noting that George Popham, a brother of the estate's owner Alexander Popham (born 1657, died 1718?), was Rector at nearby Chilton Foliat from 1714 to 1743. It is at Chilton that members of the Popham family are buried, and it is where they held patronage from 1598. Could it have belonged to him?

Amongst the finds are twenty-two farthing and halfpenny trade tokens – being illegal 'money of necessity'. Small traders and officials, due to the indifference of the government to the public's need for small change, issued them between 1648 and 1679. Details shown on the tokens would include the place of issue, the issuer's name, their trade and on the halfpenny tokens the value. The Littlecote tokens demonstrate travels to places near and far such as Malmesbury, Glastonbury, Abingdon, Bristol, Yeovil, London, Oxford, Newbury, Windsor, Wantage, Hagbourne, Speen and Wallingford. The tokens originating from Somerset may be due to the presence in that county of a further large country estate owned by the Pophams at Hunstrete, whilst those from north Berkshire are from an area in which the Pophams owned farmland. Linking some of these places is the then important coaching road (later A4) from London to Avonmouth. Travel by estate

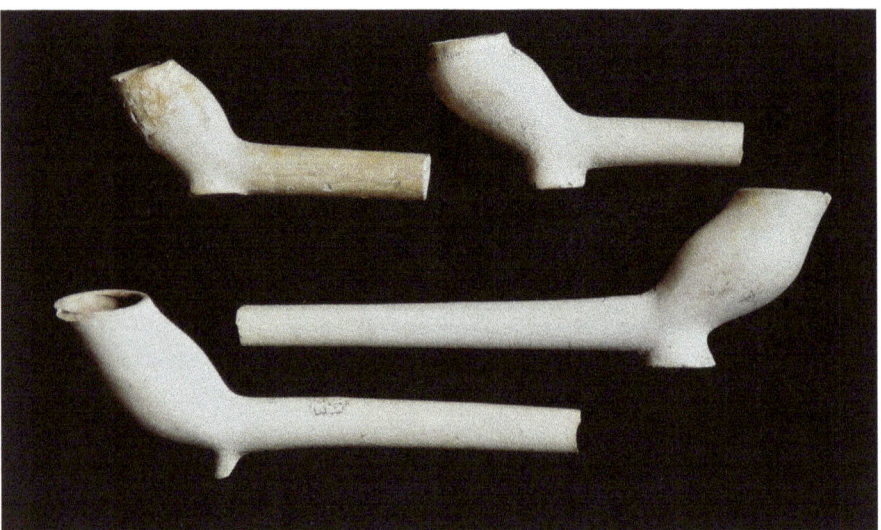

Fig. 78. Clay pipes c. 1650 to 1700 from the river

staff is noted in surviving records particularly by the estate stewards. Also, amongst the many clay pipes found, most marked with their makers name, are some from makers outside their normal distribution, like Melksham, Salisbury, and London. These places that would have to be reached by coach, cart or on horseback. Evidencing these modes of transport are horseshoes, horseshoe nails, twelve rumbler bells, bridle bits, sixteen spurs, leather reins and a linch-pin. Horse bones were also present in the river silts.

The occupants clearly had time for relaxation and amusement as revealed by various finds. Smoking, presumably for the men of the house, was clearly a major activity, as was the consumption of wine and spirits. The former is shown by the presence of the clay pipes, whilst the latter is shown by remains of at least 212 bottles, bottle corks, corkscrews, and many glass drinking vessels fragments. Music is revealed by six jaw's harps and a bone whistle, whilst gaming is hinted at by a bone counter and six copper alloy jettons. Meanwhile the ladies of the household were occupied, besides household chores, by dress and tapestry making as revealed by the bodkin, scissors, thimbles, and hundreds of dressmaking pins.

It is the c.1730 painting of Littlecote House and its grounds that provides the best indication for the appearance of the excavated cottage in its final phase. It clearly shows the structure is of two stories in the original part and the added west wing with an attic above, its rooms lit by dormer windows. Surviving structural elements demonstrate that the building's corners, apart from the probable washroom, had piers of brick whilst the walls were of flint which alternated with bands of brick. The roof, as shown by debris thrown into the river and the c. 1730 painting, was tiled in terracotta. Existing documents refer to a brickworks on the estate at Hopgrass that would have supplied bricks and tiles, whilst flints could be gleaned from the surrounding

Fig. 79. Lead strip depicting a stag's head from the rive

Fig. 80. Popham coat-of-arms

fields, and there was some evidence of stone robbing on the adjacent ancient ruins. Besides bricks and tiles, items relating to the building's construction (interior and exterior) and furniture found include iron door pivots, an iron door catch, iron hinges and an iron wall hook, bronze studs/tacks, window glass and leading, wood laths, a stone door/window reveal, a marble slab fragment, and a small stone trough. Also, present were fifteen fragments of lead strip that may have adorned wooden items, and which are decorated with stag head and floral motifs. Stag heads also feature on the Popham's coat of arms.

The river outlook provided a desirable setting, a factor not missed by the occupants who planned a garden to take advantage of it. They designed it to have cobbled areas, brick paths, screening walls, a flint-block path, flower beds and possibly an area of lawn.

An estate survey of 1775 by Thomas Smith of Shrivenham shows the cottage still standing in its final form complete with porch. Absence of pottery, clay pipes and coinage datable to after 1770-80 point to its demolition not long after the survey. A survey, c.1790, of Knighton Park, that lies on the opposite riverbank, shows several buildings on the Littlecote bank, but not the excavated building. Several other buildings visible on the c.1730 painting may also have been demolished around this time, for example a cottage in the far distance close to the river, a large gabled house on the hilltop in front of Park Coppice, and an impressive building close to Littlecote House which may have been a 'dower house'. Around the time of the cottage demolition Francis Popham, the then owner of Littlecote, had plans to build a grand house on a magnificent scale at his Hunstrete Estate in Somerset. Francis also planned a major overhaul of the Littlecote Estate at this time, or as he died in 1780 his relative who inherited the estate, also called Francis Popham, decided to make significant changes.

Could the excavated building be the estate's hunting lodge? In its true sense a hunting lodge is a building set in a hunting park erected to accommodate the requirements of participants, chiefly the gentry

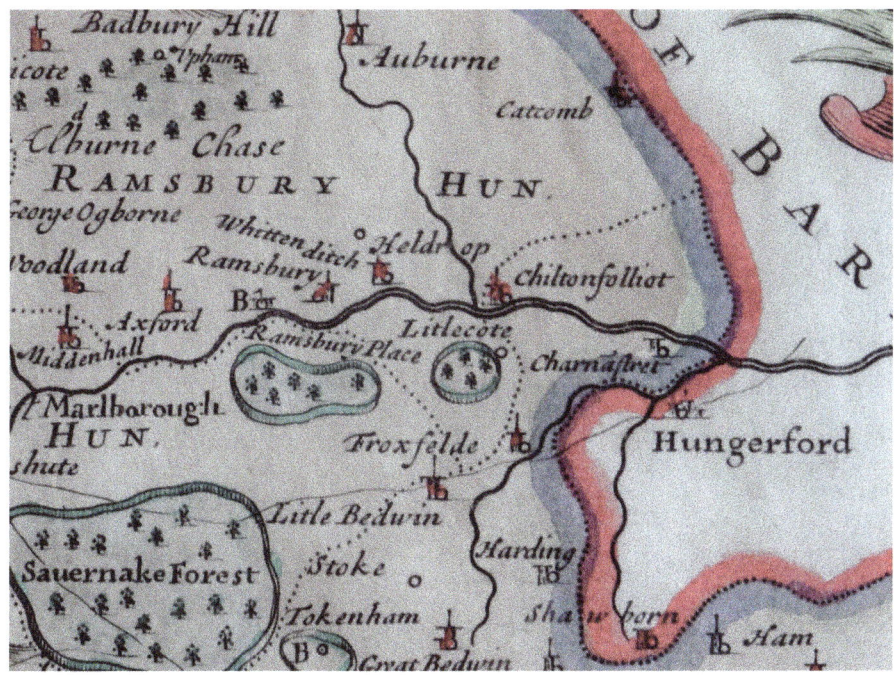

*Fig. 81. Littlecote Park shown on a map of Wiltshire by Robert Morden 1695*

engaged in the park's pursuits, whilst also being intended to house the park custodian. It is tempting to see the cottage as the estate hunting lodge but it appears, based on the finds, layout, and initial small size, to have been a family home in which aspects of hunting are apparent and which is set in a hunting park. So, who lived in the building? As previously mentioned, it is feasible that in the initial stages a river and duck decoy keeper and his family occupied the cottage. The evidence of butchery on the premises of red and roe deer, and waterfowl, along with the hunting items, also point strongly to the presence of a keeper charged with preparation of game caught on the estate intended for both the manor kitchen and for sale. However, the wealth of artefacts and structural additions, particularly the west wing and the extended garden, indicate that a person of higher standing amongst the estates workers later occupied the building. As noted above the tokens and clay pipes suggest that people in the household travelled extensively. Could it be that the house soon became the residence for the estate steward and his family? Contemporary documents record by name estate stewards who made payment for goods and services, kept accounts, and oversaw work

*Fig. 82. Littlecote Park shown on a map of Wiltshire by Andrews and Dury 1773*

etc. The stewards include Thomas Leyson in 1699, Edward Golding in 1720, William French in 1722, William George in 1733 and 1734, Thomas Hall 1728 to 1737, Charles Young in 1743, Mr Lucas in 1761 and John Deadman 1770 to 1781. The accounts also record the stewards' claims for travel undertaken on estate business, places both near and far. In 1720 they included Marlborough, Bridgwater, Hunstrete, Andover and Avebury.

It was William George who discovered Littlecote's Romano-British Orpheus mosaic in 1727. As revealed in the archaeological excavation William clearly made his discovery immediately west of the excavated cottage in an area that appears to have been the kitchen garden. If, as documents imply, William found the remains and not a lesser member of the estate staff who informed him of them, then why was he digging in the cottage garden if it was not his garden? So, William lived in the cottage. His interest in Roman remains had been

*Fig. 83. Mary George's embroidery of the Orpheus mosaic*

aroused by discoveries in 1725 of mosaics on the estate lands at Rudge Coppice and Froxfield. This may have encouraged him to dig around the cottage where undoubtedly Roman artefacts had turned up from time to time. As noted previously the unearthing of the *Orpheus* mosaic was recorded in the minutes of the Society of Antiquaries of London in April 1728. A letter written in 1729 by Mr Popham does refer to its discovery and of a visit by the Marquis of Hertford to see it. Afterwards Lord Hertford commissioned George Vertue, engraver, and antiquary (born 1683, died 1756) to produce an engraving of the mosaic. Later, William's wife Mary after her husband's death completed a very detailed embroidery of the pavement. Needlework on the embroidery reads 'this pavement is here produced was found by William George in Littlecote Park in the year of our Lord 1730 (7 foot under the surface of the earth) who dying before it was finished is by his widow made complete in this needlework...'. Several errors are evident in this statement as the mosaic, by documentary evidence, was discovered in 1727 while the 1978 excavation shows it lay only a foot below the surface. It is likely that the mosaic had remained uncovered for several years and was then deliberately reburied to prevent continuing deterioration and visitations by unwanted, inquisitive people entering the hunting park. This and her memory could have led to the mistakes by William's widow.

William George's accounts for 1733 and 1734 demonstrate that much of his work involved the overseeing of the hunting side of the estate as well as construction work that included fencing, ditching, repairs, and the sale of venison, timber, bricks, and lime. This also included paying tradesmen i.e., hay makers, mowers, a stone cutter, woodmen, and a peat-cutter. When requested he made purchases for the estate including gunpowder and shot, baskets and building material. Also, as part of his job he travelled on estate business in 1734 to Petwick near Challow, Winterbourne Monkton, Stanford in the Vale, Swindon, Pewsey, and Hungerford. William's salary is recorded in 1733 as £20 per annum.

William, son of William and Martha George was baptised on the 3rd of May 1697 in Froxfield. He had eight siblings also baptised in Froxfield – John in 1698, Richard 1701, Joseph 1704, Mary 1706, Matthew 1708, Michael 1713, Anne 1715, and Benjamin 1717. Froxfield was part of the Littlecote Estate at this period, and it is possible that the father, if this is the right family, worked on the Estate. A marriage licence bond had been obtained for William George bachelor and Mary Moore spinster both of Ramsbury in 1728. The excavated cottage lies in Ramsbury Parish. William's marriage is not listed in the Parish registers, but they must have married somewhere for in 1731 a son of William and Mary was baptised in Ramsbury Church. A daughter Mary followed in 1733 and another Hannah was born in 1737. It could be that they married in Littlecote's chapel. It is unknown where and when William died since a search of local registers has proved negative. Yet his widow must have retained a connection with Littlecote as the tapestry she produced of the mosaic was until recently kept there.

Although it was an isolated structure in the landscape, the excavated cottage was clearly a functional element in the much larger picture of the 260-acre hunting park. Littlecote was an estate dedicated to the hunting pursuits of the wealthy, as well portrayed in the c.1730 painting. Besides those already mentioned, further elements of the hunting park are recorded on eighteenth century maps and surveys, on the painting and by present day observations. Included are the park pale, park ditch, watchtower, icehouse, ha-ha, stables and various lodges. Documents of the period show items such as in 1734 of 'payment to Thomas Morse for mending the bullet gun for Pope', in 1738 'for slitting and edging a parcel of slabs to mend the park pale' and in 1783 'for two bucks brought in that escaped out of the hunting'.

Clearly the Popham family were people of high status both in their possessions and social standing. Francis Popham (born 1573, died 1644) was the owner of Littlecote Estate from 1607 and was during his lifetime a soldier, Member of Parliament, Justice of the Peace, Deputy Lieutenant for Wilts and Somerset, Knight of the Bath, and Constable of Taunton Castle. Following his death his son Alexander (born 1605, died 1669) became owner of Littlecote. Like his father he was a Member of Parliament, Justice of the Peace, and participated in the military, most notably during the English Civil War, when he fought for Parliament, having the rank of Colonel. After the restoration of the Monarchy, he made his peace with Charles II and entertained him to a "costlie dinner" at Littlecote. Following Alexander's death, his son Francis (born 1645, died 1674) took over the estate and was succeeded by his son Alexander (born 1669, died 1705) who died without having children. The estate

*Fig. 84. Alexander Popham (1605-1669) and his family*

then passed to his uncle, also called Alexander (born 1657, died 1718(?)). Francis (born 1682, died 1735) owner of Littlecote after his father's death became a Member of Parliament. His son Edward (born 1709, died 1772), who took over the estate, also became a Member of Parliament. Francis his son (born 1734, died 1780) married Dorothy Hutton, daughter of the Archbishop of Canterbury, but they had no children together.

---

*For further information on the Pophams and other owners of Littlecote see 'Littlecote, Lives and Legends – The Story of a Great Estate and its Famous Families' by Pauline Mobey, People and Places ((pauline.mobey@people-and-places.info).*

# References

Braithwaite, G., 1984: Romano-British face pots and head pots, *Britannia*, volume XV, pp. 99-131

Chadwick Hawkes, S., 1961: Soldiers and Settlers in Britain, Fourth to Fifth Century, *Medieval Archaeology*, volume 9, pp. 1-70

Chapelot and Fossier, 1985: *The Village and House in the Middle Ages*, University of California Press

Cosh, S. R., 2001: Seasonal Dining Rooms in Romano-British Houses, *Britannia*, volume XXXII, pp. 219-238

Croucher, B., 1986: *The Village in the Valley*, privately printed, Ramsbury.

Crowley, D. A., 1983: 'Ramsbury' in *A History of Wiltshire, The Victoria History of the Counties of England;* volume XII, Oxford University Press

Cunliffe, B., 2013: *The Roman Villa at Brading, Isle of White: The Excavations of 2008-10*, Oxford University School of Archaeology, Monograph

Dyer, C., 1995: Sheepcotes: evidence for Medieval Sheep Farming, *Medieval Archaeology*, volume 39, pp. 136-164

Ellis, S. P., 1995: Classical Reception Rooms in Romano-British Houses, *Britannia*, volume XXVI, pp 163-178

Gentry, A. P., 1976: Roman Military Stone-Built Granary in Britain, *British Archaeological Reports*, British Series 32

Gilchrist, R., 2012: *Medieval Life, Archaeology and the Life Course*, Boydell Press, Woodbridge

Griffiths, N., 2001: 'The Roman Army in Wiltshire' in P. Ellis (edit), *Roman Wiltshire and After*, Wiltshire Archaeological and Natural History Society

Halbaek, H., 1964: The Isca Grain; a Roman Plant Introduction to Britain, *New Phytologist*, volume 63, pp. 158-164

Harvey, P. D. A., 1993: Rectitudines Singularum Personarum and Gerefa, The English Historical Review, volume 108, No. 426 (Jan.), pp. 1-22, Oxford University Press

Hill, C., 2003: *Origins of the English*, London

Locker, A., 2007: In piscibus diversis; the Bone Evidence for Fish Consumption in Roman Britain, Britannia, volume 38, pp. 141-180

MacGregor, A., 1985: *Bone, Antler, Ivory and Horn: The Technology of Skeletal Materials since the Roman Period*. Croom Helm

Mepham, L. N., 1993: 'The Fired Clay', pp. 34 and 'The Worked Bone', pp. 40. in Graham, A. and Newham, C., Recent Excavations of Iron Age and Romano-British Enclosures in the Avon Valley, Wiltshire, *Wiltshire Archaeological and Natural History Magazine*, volume 86

Mepham, L. and Heaton, M., 1995: A Medieval Pottery Kiln at Ashampstead,

Berkshire, *Medieval Ceramic*, volume 19, pp. 29-43

Moorhead, T. S. N., 2001: 'Roman Coin Finds from Wiltshire' in P. Ellis, (edit): *Roman Wiltshire and After*, Wiltshire Archaeological and Natural History Society

Morris. J. 1979: *Domesday Book – Wiltshire*, Phillimore

Morris, P., 1979: *Agricultural Buildings in Roman Britain*, British Archaeological Reports, British Series 70

Musty, J., 1973: A Preliminary Account of a Medieval Pottery Industry at Minety, North Wiltshire, *Wiltshire Archaeological and Natural History Magazine*, volume 68, pp. 79-88

Pearce, J. and Vince, A., 1988: *Surrey Whitewares*, London and Middlesex Archaeological Society, Special Paper Number 10

Reynolds, P.J. and Langly, J.K., 1979: 'Romano-British corn-drying ovens: an experiment' *Archaeological Journal*, volume 136, pp. 27-42

Rivet, A. L. F., 1964: *Town and Country in Roman Britain*, (2nd edition), London

Smith, D. J., 1978: 'Regional aspects of the winged corridor house' in Todd, M., (edit) *Studies in the Romano-British Villa*, Leicester University Press, pp. 117-147

Stevens, C. J., 2011: Charred plant remains from Springhead in Barnett, C., McKinley, J.I., Stafford, E., Grimm, J.M. and Stevens, C.J., *Settling the Ebbsfleet Valley, High Speed 1 Excavations at Springhead and Northfleet, Kent: The Late Iron Age, Roman, Saxon and Medieval Landscape, volume 3: Late Iron Age to Roman human remains and environmental reports*, pp. 95-105, Oxford/Salisbury, Oxford Wessex Archaeology Report

Stratton, J. M., 1978: *Agricultural Records AD 220-1978*, John Barker

Walters, B., 1984: The Orpheus Mosaic in Littlecote Park, Wiltshire, R. Faroli Campati (ed.), *Il mosaico antico (III Colloquio Internazionale sul mosaico antico)*, Rome

Witts, P., 2000: Mosaics and Room Function: Fourth Century Romano-British Villas, *Britannia*, volume XXXI

# Glossary

**Advowson** – in ecclesiastical law, the right to make an appointment of a member of the clergy to a living.
**Annona militaris** – the Roman Emperor Septimius Severus established this to meet the dietary needs of the army, a sort of tax paid in kind. It started as an exceptional measure and then a recurrent one, until it became a property tax in kind.
**Apollo** – a Greek god who was associated with the bow, music, and divination. The epitome of youth and beauty, source of life and healing, patron of the civilized arts, and as bright and powerful as the sun itself.
**Apple corer** – a device for removing the core and pips from an apple.
**Bacchus** – the Roman god of agriculture, wine, and fertility, equivalent to the Greek god Dionysus. The Dionysian/Bacchic Mysteries were a ritual of ancient Greece and Rome which sometimes used intoxicants and other trance-inducing techniques (like dance and music) to remove inhibitions and social constraints, liberating the individual to return to a natural state.
**Bobbin** – a cylinder holding thread or yarn used especially in weaving.
**Bottle seal** – a seal consisted of a molten blob of glass which the glass blower placed on the shoulder of a bottle and impressed it with a circular seal *matrix*. Inscribed on this seal matrix was usually a name or initials and sometimes a date or crest.
**Bowl furnace** – a shallow clay-lined hollow dug into the ground into which bellows pumped air through a tuyere (clay pipe) to raise the temperature using charcoal as fuel to enable the smelting of iron ore placed within it.
**Butter pat** – a flat paddle-like wood implement used to form blocks of butter.
**Byre** – a farm building or part of a building for the housing of cattle.
**Cess pit** – a hollow in the ground dug to contain human waste. Often the walls were lined but not floored to allow fluids to soak away.
**Costrel** – a flat, usually earthenware, container for liquids having loops for a belt or a cord for carrying.
**Cresset lamp** – a pottery lamp having a spiked base that fitted into a looped iron holder set into a timber beam.
**Cross passage** – a route between two opposing external doors within a medieval building.
**Crucible** – a vessel made from materials that can resist extreme temperatures and used for extremely hot processes such as melting metals.
**Crucible furnace** – a simple construction employed to melt metal using extreme heat and a crucible.
**Dea Nutrix** – the Roman Mother Goddess, whose little effigies are a common

find on Roman sites throughout Roman Britain and the Roman Empire. Usually portrayed as a young woman sitting in a wicker chair, holding a baby to each breast.

**Demeter** – the Greek goddess of the harvest and agriculture, presiding over grains and the fertility of the earth. Identified as Ceres in Roman religion she was the mother of Persephone. On the Littlecote mosaic she is depicted as autumn and maturity and holds a vine staff. She dances in front of a bull.

**Dionysus** – the ancient Greek god of wine, winemaking, grape cultivation, fertility, ritual madness, theatre, and religious ecstasy. He was the son of Zeus and Persephone.

**Dobunni** – an Iron Age tribe that occupied an area centred on Gloucestershire, with their pre-Roman capital probably in the fortified settlement at Bagendon near Cirencester.

**Dovecote** – a structure to house doves or pigeons. They may be free-standing structures in a variety of shapes or built into the end of a house or barn. They generally contain pigeonholes for the birds to nest in.

**Dower house** – a moderately large house available for use by the widow of the previous owner of the estate.

**Dwarf wall** – a low wall often constructed to support an upper structure which in ancient times could be a timber frame with wattle and daub infill. Such a wall protected the timbers from rising damp and thus resulting rot.

**Encaustic tiles** – terracotta tiles that have a pattern or figure impressed into their upper surface and with that impression being infilled with a coloured clay differing to that of the tile's body. The tiles upper surface is then usually coated in a clear glaze.

**Fortuna** – the goddess of fortune – good or bad – and the personification of luck in Roman religion.

**Foundation beam** – a timber beam set into the ground to support an upper timber structure.

**Fuller** – a person who thickens cloth, by matting the fibres together to give it strength and increase waterproofing (felting).

**Fuller's earth** – a clay-like substance that is mostly composed of aluminium magnesium silicate. This name comes from its use by fullers to remove dirt and oil from wool.

**Furlong** – a measure of distance in imperial units equal to one eighth of a mile, equivalent to 660 feet, 220 yards, 40 rods, 10 chains or approximately 201 metres

**Garter hook** – a metal hook sewn onto the end of a cloth ribbon which wrapped around a leg supporting a stocking in place. The hook was inserted into the ribbon to keep it tight around the leg. They also served a similar function when attached to the end of leg wraps common in the early medieval period.

**Granary** – a building or room (usually in a barn) that holds grain. It keeps the grain dry so it does not spoil and keeps it away from pests that would eat it.

**Gun flint** – the shaped piece of flint that provides the igniting spark in a flintlock weapon.

**Ha-ha** – an architectural landscape feature in the grounds of an English country house. It comprises a ditch with on one side a vertical retaining wall which prevented sheep and other livestock from entering the gardens of the house but does not spoil the views from the house of the surrounding countryside.

**Hillfort** – an enclosure surrounded by defensive ditches and banks, often built on hill tops in the Late Bronze Age and Iron Age periods.

**Hostelry** – a building providing food and accommodation.

**Hypocaust** – a system of central heating in a building that produces and circulates hot air below the floor of a room and warms the walls by a series of pipes through which the hot air passes.

**Icehouse** – a building used to store ice throughout the year prior to the invention of the refrigerator. Many were man-made underground chambers that were situated close to natural sources of winter ice such as medieval fishponds and freshwater lakes.

**Intaglio** – a design incised or engraved into a material.

**Jaw's harp** – (or jew's harp) a metal or wood lyre-shaped musical instrument that is held sideways between the teeth. When a central metal tongue is struck, twitched, or twanged it produce a twanging sound that can be changed by altering the shape of the mouth cavity and moving the tongue.

**Jettons** – thin copper coin-like tokens produced and used throughout Europe between the thirteenth and seventeenth centuries. Originally made for use in calculating, they later served as a money substitute in gaming.

**Latch lifter** – a primitive key comprising a very simple metal shaft with a hook or a couple of teeth on the end. In use it was to pass through a hole in a door and fit into a latch to lift and move it.

**Leda** – a figure from Greek mythology who was famously seduced by Zeus when he took the form of a swan. She was a queen of Sparta and mother of beautiful Helen who sparked the Trojan War. On the Littlecote mosaic she or Nemesis is depicted as summer and youth and holds a swan (it is not certain of the two who this figure represents). She dances in front of a panther.

**Long hearth** – a long tunnel-like clay construction, open at one end with a fire pit at the other. This enabled smoke from a fire to travel along the tunnel and ascend at the other as cooled smoke, an important factor in preserving food in a smokehouse.

**Longhouse** – a single-floored building usually consisting of a range of three rooms – a bedroom, living room and a byre or service room, the latter separated from the living area by a cross passage.

**Linch-pin** – a metal fastener used to prevent a cart or carriage wheel from sliding off the axle on which it is riding on.

**Malt** – a product from grain of starch, enzymes, protein, vitamins, and minerals plus many other minor constituents that provide the brewer and distiller with their main raw material.

**Malt house** – a building in which malt is prepared and stored.

**Malting hearth/kiln/oven** – a fire source over which sprouted grains cold be spread on a platform above. Initially a gentle fire would have been started and gradually increased over two to four days to suit the malt's purpose and the desired colour.

**Mason** – a skilled person who works with different types of materials including brick, tile, and stone to build structures.

**Midden** – a dump of domestic rubbish or animal waste that has built up over time.

**Millstone** – a large flat circular stone, one of a pair, used in a mill to grind grain into flour.

**Nemesis** – the ancient Greek goddess of divine retribution. As such she meted out punishment for evil deeds, undeserved good fortune, and hubris (arrogance before the gods).

**Opus signinum** – a waterproof building material used in Roman times. It is made of terracotta tiles broken up into very small pieces, mixed with mortar.

**Orpheus** – a legendary musician, poet, and prophet in ancient Greek religion. He is often pictured playing a lyre. Orpheus's music also tamed Cerberus the monstrous three-headed dog who guarded the gates of the underworld.

**Pattens** – protective wooden overshoes set on an iron ring and held in place by leather or cloth bands. They were worn to raise one's feet above wet or muddy ground.

**Penannular brooch** – a dress fastener comprising a metal circular band interrupted by a slot, and to which is attached a moveable metal pin.

**Persephone** – also known as Kore, the daughter of Zeus and Demeter and the mother of Zagreus. She became the queen of the Underworld through her abduction by Hades, God of the underworld. She was the personification of vegetation which shoots forth in spring and withdraws into the earth after harvest. On the Littlecote mosaic she is depicted as winter and death waving farewell as she enters the underworld. She dances in front of a goat.

**Pipe Rolls** – the oldest and longest series of English public records and a valuable source for the financial and administrative history of medieval England.

**Porringer** – a metal, wood or earthen ware vessel having a single or two opposing flat horizontal handles and used for soup, stew, or similar food.

**Pseudo villa** – a timber farmhouse having pretentions of grandeur.

**Quern** – two mounted circular stones, the lower having a convex upper surface and the upper an opposing concave surface and a central hole. When the upper stone was rotated grain fed through the hole was ground into flour.

**Samian** – red or rarely black earthenware pottery having a glossy finish made on Gaulish potteries from the first century BC to the mid-third century AD.

**Sarsen stone** – a silicified sandstone boulder of a kind which occurs on the chalk downs of southern England.

**Shaft furnace** – a vertical cylindrical clay shaft in which extreme heat produces liquid metals by the reaction of a flow of air introduced under pressure into the bottom of the shaft with a mixture of metallic ore and charcoal fed into the top.

**Shake** – a basic wooden shingle (see below) made from split logs used to cover roofs.

**Sheepcote** – a large late medieval building used for winter shelter of sheep, as a fodder store, and during lambing.

**Shingle** – thin, tapered pieces of cut wood, primarily used to cover roofs and walls of buildings to protect them from the weather.

**Slave mill** – a pair of large rotary grinding stones (see quern) operated by man or animal power.

**Smithing hearth/blacksmith's hearth** – the source in which the smith heats up a billet of iron produced in a smelting furnace to enable hammering, to remove excess slag and trapped air and then heat up the iron so that it can be shaped with hand tools into the required form.

**Sol** – the personification of the Sun and a god in ancient Roman religion.

**Stylus** – a short thin metal rod pointed for writing at one end and flattened at the other for erasing. It was used to write in a thin wax layer held in two recessed wooden panels hinged together, which when closed protected the written message.

**Sunken-floored building** – or a sunken-featured building is a structure that is constructed within a large rectangular flat-bottomed hollow.

**Thread picker** – a bone or antler cylindrical implement having points at each end. They were used on a warp-weighted loom to straighten threads that may have stuck together as the weaving progressed.

**Trade tokens** – illegal 'money of necessity'. Small traders and officials due to the indifference of the government to the public's need for small change issued them between 1648 and 1679. Details shown on the tokens would include the place of issue, the issuer's name, and their trade.

**Tufa** – porous rock composed of calcium carbonate and formed by precipitation from water e.g., around mineral springs.

**Venus** – in Roman mythology the goddess of love, sex, beauty, and fertility and the counterpart to the Greek goddess Aphrodite. On the Littlecote mosaic she is depicted as spring and birth and holds a mirror. She dances in front of a deer.

**Victoria** – the Roman goddess of victory who was closely related with the Roman military.

**Wattle and daub** – a form of walling that consists of a woven lattice of trimmed branches or wooden strips daubed with a sticky material, usually made from a combination of wet soil, clay, sand, animal dung and straw.

**Wig curlers** – short fired white clay rods with bulbous ends. Heated up and wrapped in paper they were used to set curls in wigs during the eighteenth century.

**Wool comb** – an iron toothed implement used for processing wool by disentangling, cleaning and intermixing fibres prior to spinning.

**Zagreus-Bacchus** – Zagreus is an Underworld God of hunting and rebirth and the son of Hades and Persephone. He was later equated with the Orphic Dionysus/Bacchus.

# People and Places Index

Abingdon 102
Ald Valley 9
Allectus 46
Andover 106
Andrews and Dury map 96, 106
Angles 56
Anglo-Saxon 57, 58, 81
Anne, Queen 94
Antinous 45-6
Apollo 44, 113
Arcadius 50
Archbishop of Canterbury 110
Argonne 18
Ashampstead, near Reading 84
Avebury 106
Avon and Somerset 30, 81
Avonmouth 102

Bacchic 45, 46, 48
Bacchus 44-6, 48, 113, 118
Bacchus-Antinous 46
Barbury Castle 57
Bear Inn, Hungerford 99
Berkshire 1, 84, 102
Bigg, Mr 83
Bishop of Salisbury 60
Brading, Isle of Wight 24
Bridgwater 106
Bristol 102
Britain 7, 8, 13, 20, 21, 34, 37, 55, 56, 85
British 6, 29, 37, 38, 56, 58
Bronze Age, Late 6, 115

Caligula 10
*Calleva Atrebatum* 9, 17
Calstone, Roger de (1) 61

Calstone, Roger de (2) 61
Calstone, Elizabeth de 62
Calstone, Joan de 61
Calstone, Lawrence de 61-2
Calstone, Sir Lawrence de 61-2
Calstone, Thomas 61-2
*Camulodunum* 8
Canterbury, Archbishop of 110
Catuvellaunian 8
Celtic 55
Central Gaulish 28
Charles II 94, 109
Chesters fort 35
Chilton Foliat 27, 59, 102
Christ 28
Christianity 28, 46
Cirencester (*Corinium*) 9, 45
Civil War, English 92, 109
Claudian/Neronian 10
Claudius 8, 10
Colchester (*Camulodunum*) 8
Cologne 18
Constans 42, 43, 46
Constantine 42
Constantinian 43, 46
Constantius II 43, 44, 46
Constantine III 55
Corinium 9, 45
Cosh, S R 48
Cowley, Thomas 83
*Cvnetio* 9, 17, 50

Darrell, Sir George 62, 90
Darrell, William, 62
Deadman, John 106
Demeter 44, 113, 116
Diocletian 37

Dionysus 45, 113, 114, 118
Dixon, Samuel 95
Dobunnic 9, 10
Domesday Book 58, 59, 83
Durnford, Richard of 61
Durnford, Roger of 61
*Durocornovium* 9

Early Iron Age 6
Early Medieval 55-8
Edward III 61, 81
Elizabeth I 101
Ellis, S P 48
England 62, 86, 116
English Civil War 92, 109
English School 91, 95
Europe 64, 94, 115

Fortuna 28, 114
French, William 106
Frocester Court 30
Froxfield 108

Gaul 13, 29, 55
Gaulish 18, 28, 55, 116
George II 94, 101
George, Anne 108
George, Benjamin 108
George, Hannah 109
George, John 108
George, Joseph 108
George, Martha 108
George, Mary (1) 108
George, Mary, nee Moore (2) 107, 109
George, Matthew 108
George, Michael 108
George, Richard 108
George, William (1) 109
George, William (2) ix, 1, 3, 106, 108, 109
Germanic 55-7
Gildas 56-7
Glastonbury 102

Golding, Edward 106
Gratian 55
Greek 28, 44, 45, 113-17

Hadrian 26, 46
Hadrian's Wall 16, 35
Hagbourne 102
Hall, Thomas 106
Henry VIII 62, 90
Hertford, Marquis of 2, 108
Hoger, Johann Conrad 94
Honorius 50-1
Hopgrass 103
Hungerford 99, 108
Hunstrete 102, 104, 106
Hutton, Dorothy 110

Ireland 55
Iron Age 6, 56, 114, 115

Julian the Apostate 46, 48
Jutes 56

Kennet, River 1, 2, 4, 6, 17, 50, 60, 80, 83, 85, 95
Kennet Valley 8, 9, 57, 84
Knighton Park 96, 104

Late Bronze Age 6, 115
Laverstock 84
Leda 44, 115
Legion II Augusta 8-9
Leverton 59
Leyson, Thomas 106
Liddington Castle 56-7
Littlecote Estate 1, 2, 90, 91, 99, 105-10
Littlecote Estate Accounts and Survey 85, 95-6, 104
Littlecote House 1, 2, 60, 86, 90, 91, 103
Littlecote Park 1, 90, 91, 95, 97, 104-9

Londinium 50
London 2, 50, 79, 102, 103, 108
Lower Wanborough vii, ix-xii, 9
Lucas, Mr 106
Luttrell Psalter 80
Lyveden, Northamptonshire 85

Magnus Maximus 55
Malmesbury 102
Marcus 55
Marlborough 106
Medieval 3, 14, 26, 33, 36, 55, 58, 60-4, 69, 80-6, 91, 96, 113-17
Melksham 103
Mesolithic 7
Mildenhall 9, 17, 50
Minety 84
Moorhead, T S N 50
Morden, Robert 105
Morse, Thomas 109
Much Hadham, Hertfordshire 45

Naish Hill 84
Nene Valley 29
Neolithic 6, 7
New Forest 38, 53
Newbury 84, 102
Nile, River 46
North Gaulish 18
North Leigh 30
North Wiltshire 29, 84
Nuremberg 94

Orpheus 41, 43-5, 95, 106-8, 116
Orphic 39-47, 49, 51, 118
Oxford 101, 102
Oxfordshire 30, 38

Park Coppice 104
Persephone 44, 114, 116, 118
Petwick near Challow 108
Pewsey 108
Phillips, Bernard vii-xv, 1-3

Phillips, Roger x, xv
Phillips, Thomas 95
Pictish 55
Pipe Rolls 61, 116
Pleistocene 5
Popham family 99, 102, 104, 109
Popham, Alexander (1605 - 1669) 109
Popham, Alexander (1669 - 1705) 109
Popham, Alexander (1657 - 1718?) 99, 102, 110
Popham, Edward (1709 - 1772) 110
Popham, Francis (1573-1644) 109
Popham, Francis (1645 - 1674) 109
Popham, Francis (1682 - 1735) ix, 99, 110
Popham, Francis (1734 - 1780)
Popham, George 102
Post-Roman 52, 53, 56
Pyrmont, Waldeck, Germany 99
Pyrmont Water 99

Queen Anne 94

Ramsbury 61, 90, 109
Ramsbury Church 109
Ramsbury Hundred 58, 60, 83
Ramsbury Parish 109
Reading 4, 17, 84
Richard II 69, 85
River Kennet 1, 2, 4, 6, 17, 50, 60, 80, 83, 85, 95
River Nile 46
River Thames 4, 17, 57, 79
Roman Britain 20, 21, 37, 113
Romano-British 44, 57, 63, 81, 106
Roman Empire 44, 113
Roman Research Trust 3
Rome 55, 113
Rudge Coppice 108

Salisbury 60, 103

Salisbury, Bishop of 60
Samian ware 10, 18, 28, 38, 116
Savary, Mr Peter de xiii, 3
Saxon 55-8
Seymour, Jane 62
Shrivenham 96, 104
Silchester 9, 17
Smith, Thomas 96, 104
Society of Antiquaries 2, 108
Sol 27-8, 117
Somerset 30, 81, 102, 104, 109
Southern Britain 8
Southern Spain 29
Speen 17, 102
*Spinis* 17
Stanford in the Vale 108
Stanton Fitzwarren vii, x
Surrey/Hampshire border 84
Swindon vii-xi, 108

Taunton Castle 109
Thames, River 4, 17, 57, 79
Thames Valley 57
Trier 28
Tudor 1

*Urbs Roma* 43

Valentinianic 50
Venus 44, 117
Vertue, George ix, 2, 108
Vespasian 8
Victoria 28, 117
*Vindolanda* 16
Vitruvius 24

Wallingford 102
Walters, Bryn ix-xv, 1-3, 46
Wanborough (Durocornovium) vii, ix-xii, 9
Wantage 102
Warner Leisure Hotels 1
West Saxon Bishopric 58
West Whelpington 85
Westbury, Buckinghamshire 85
Wills, Sir David Seton xii-xiii, 2, 3
Windsor 102
Winterbourne Monkton 108
Witts, P 48

Yeovil 102
Young, Charles 106

Zagreus-Bacchus 116, 118

www.ingramcontent.com/pod-product-compliance
Lightning Source LLC
Chambersburg PA
CBHW050032090426
42735CB00022B/3461